William Sharp

The Gypsy Christ

And other Tales

William Sharp

The Gypsy Christ
And other Tales

ISBN/EAN: 9783337074500

Printed in Europe, USA, Canada, Australia, Japan

Cover: Foto ©ninafisch / pixelio.de

More available books at **www.hansebooks.com**

The Gypsy Christ

And Other Tales

BY

WILLIAM SHARP

CHICAGO
STONE & KIMBALL
M DCCC XCV

TO

LADY COLIN CAMPBELL

FROM HER FRIEND
THE AUTHOR OF THESE DIVERS TALES OF
DIVERS LANDS

Contents

THE GYPSY CHRIST	3
MADGE O' THE POOL	75
THE COWARD	129
A VENETIAN IDYL	171
THE GRAVEN IMAGE	215
THE LADY IN HOSEA	237
FRÖKEN BERGLIOT	255

THE GYPSY CHRIST.

The Gypsy Christ.

I.

THERE are, among the remote uplands of the Peak district, regions whose solitude is that of a wilderness. Over much of the country there is a frown. When fair weather prevails: though these lofty plateaux are seldom wholly free from cloud-shadow: this frown is merely that of a stern man, preoccupied with sombre thoughts. When there come rain and wind, and still more the dull absorbing gloom that floods out of the east and the north-east, the frown is forbidding, minatory even, at times almost tragic. Viewed anywhere from High Peak to Sir William, these uplands are like the sea. They reach onward, lapse, merge into each other, in a similar succession of vast billows: grand as they, as apparently limitless, and, at times, as overwhelmingly depressing.

The villages are scattered, insignificant: built of dull, grey stone: gardenless, flowerless. The people are uncouth in speech and manner: cold, too, as the stone of their houses, and strangely quiet in the ordinary expression of emotion.

In all regions where the wind is the paramount feature in the duel between man and the powers of nature, as upon the seas and great moorland tracts, it is noticeable that human voices are pitched in an unusually low key. In remote islands, upon mountains, on the billows of hill-land that sweep up from the plains and fall away in dales and valleys, on long flats of grass, fen, or morass, and upon the seas, the human voice takes to itself in time a peculiar, and to those who know the cause, a strangely impressive hush. Here, it is as of men subdued, but resentful, forever gloomful.

No land is so dreary as to be without redeeming beauty. The hill-region of the Peak, that most visited at any rate, has singular charm. The dales are famous for their loveliness, their picturesqueness; the heather slopes for their blithe air; the high moors for their wide perspectives, their clear windy breath, their glory of light and shadow. Nevertheless, there are vast districts where nature, and man, and the near way and the wide prospect, and the very immensity of the environing sky, are permeated with the inner spirit of gloom, as the cloud-caravans of July with their burden of thunder.

There are reasons why I do not wish to be explicit topographically, in what I am about to narrate: indeed, no one from what I write, could find the Wood o' Wendray, or the House o' Fanshawe. It must suffice, that what I have to tell occurred in the remotest, perhaps the grandest, certainly to me the most impressive region of the Peak-Land.

Far among these uplands; at the locality I mean, from twelve or fifteen hundred to two thousand feet above the sea; there is an almost trackless morass, called Grailph Moss.

The name is by some supposed to be a corruption of grey wolf: for here, according to rumour, the last wolf in England had its lair, and might have been living still (for the huntsmen aver that the grey wolf lives three hundred years!) but for its audacity at the time of the Great Plague. Packmen and other wayfarers have alleged that on wild nights of storm, or in even more perilous seasons of mist or marsh-fog, they have seen a gaunt shape leap towards them from a dense clump of heather or from behind a juniper, or have heard, behind or in stealthy circuit, terrifying footfalls as of a huge dog.

Grailph Moss comes right upon an old disused highway. Along this road, at far intervals, are desolate hamlets: in all save the three summer months, apt to be isled in the mist breathed from the myriad nostrils of the great Fen. At these times, the most dreadful thing to endure is the silence.

Not far from one of these hamlets, and somewhat more removed from the contagion of the Moss: high-set, indeed, and healthy, if sombre of aspect save under the fugitive bloom of the afterglow, or where redeemed by the moonlight to an austere beauty: is a strange house, the strangest I have seen anywhere.

The House o' Fanshawe, it is called in the neighbourhood: though what is perplexing is that the name is centuries old, though for centuries no family of that name occupied the Manor of Eastrigg: nor is there any local legend concerning a Fanshawe, or record of any kind to account for the persistency of the designation.

Long before my friend, James Fanshawe, took the Manor, ruin had come upon the middle as well as the northern portion. In fact, the southern end, which had been the original Elizabethan house, was scarce better, and had been preserved at all only because of its fantastic, often beautiful, and always extraordinary roof and wainscot carvings. These were none the less striking from the fact that they were whitewashed. Many were in a fashion suggestive of the Arabesques of Barbary, such as are to be seen to this day in the private houses of the rich Moors of Tlemçen or Tunis. Others recalled the freaks of the later Renaissance imagination: and some were of Gothic rudeness and vigor. But the most extraordinary room of all was a small chamber opening from a large vaulted apartment. All the panels on three sides of the room, and the whole roof, were covered with arabesques of the Crucifixion: no one whitewashed carving quite like any other, though all relentlessly realistic, sometimes savagely, brutally so. The fourth side was of varnished black oak. Against this, in startling relief, was a tall white cross, set in a black stand; with a drooping and terrible figure of the crucified God, the more painfully arresting from the fact that the substance of which it had been wrought had been dyed a vivid scarlet, that, with time, had become blood-red.

A word as to how I came to know this house in this remote and desolate region.

Two or three years ago, when wandering afoot through Croatia, I encountered James Fanshawe. There is no need to narrate what led up to our strange meeting, for a strange meeting in strange circumstances, and in a strange place, it was. It will suffice for me to say that our encounter, our voluntary acquaintanceship, and our subsequent friendship, all arose from the circumstance that each of us could, with more justice than some who have done so, claim to be a Romany Rye — which is not exactly "a gentleman-gypsy," as commonly translated, but rather an amateur-gypsy, or as a "brother" once phrased it to me "a sympathising make-believe gypsy." There are some who can talk the dialects of "Little Egypt," or at least understand them, and many who know something of the folk-lore, habits, and customs of the wandering people: but there are few, I take it, who have lived the gypsy-life — who have undergone, or even heard of, the ordeal of the Blue Smoke, the Two Fires, and the Running Water.

Thereafter, we met on several occasions: frequently in Italy, or the Tyrol, or southern Germany: generally by pre-arrangement. The last time I saw Fanshawe, until I met him in Glory Woods, near Dorking, was in the Hohenheim country, on the high plateau to the southwest of Stuttgart. It was then he told me he had been to England, and had travelled afoot from Southampton to Hull: and that he had at last decided to settle in that country, probably in the New Forest region. I promised to visit him in England when next there. I wanted to fare awhile with him there and then, but as it was clear he did not at that juncture wish my company, I forbore.

James Fanshawe was a noticeable man. Tall, sinewy, ruddy though with dark, luminous eyes, and long, trailing, coal-black moustache, he would not have seemed more than thirty years old but for his iron-gray hair, and the deep crow's feet about his mouth, eyes, and temples. As a matter of fact, he was, at the time I first met him, at the Midsummer's-day of human life; for he had just entered his fortieth year.

One early spring day, when, by the merest hazard, we came across each other in Glory Woods, he reminded me that nearly two years had passed since my promise to visit him. He had not, after all, settled in the south country, but, he told me, in a strange old house, in a remote and wild moorland tract of Derbyshire. While he spoke, I was observant of the great change in him. He had grown ten, fifteen years older in appearance. The iron-gray hair had become white; the strong face, rigid; the swift, alert look now that of a visionary, or of one who brooded much. Perhaps the most marked change was in the eyes. What had always struck me as their dusky, velvety Czech beauty was no longer noticeable. They were much lighter, and had a strange, staring intensity.

But I was glad to see him again: glad to pick up lost clues, and glad to be able to promise to be with him at Eastrigg Manor at the end of the sixth week from that date.

That is how I came to know the "House o' Fanshawe."

II.

EASTRIGG itself is more than twenty miles from the nearest station. The drive thence seemed the longer and drearier because of the wet mist which hung over the country. Even sounds were soaked up by it. I never passed through a drearier land. Mid-April, and not a green thing visible, not a bird's note audible!

The driver of the gig was taciturn, yet could not quite restrain his curiosity. He was not an Eastrigg man, but knew the place, and all connected with it. He would fain have ascertained somewhat about its owner; perhaps, too, about myself, or at any rate about my object in coming to the reputed haunted, if not accursed House o' Fanshawe, where my host-to-be lived alone, attended only by an old man named Hoare, a "foreigner" too, because come from the remote south country. When, however, he found me even more reserved than himself, he desisted from further inquiry, or indeed remarks of any kind.

It was in silence that we drove the last ten miles; in silence that we jolted along a rude, grassy highway of olden days, heavily rutted; in silence that we passed, first one, then another gaunt ruin,—two of the many long-deserted lead-mine chimneys which stand here and there throughout that country, and add unspeakably to its desolation. Finally, in silence we reached the House o' Fanshawe.

A small side-door, under heavy beams, opened. An elderly man stood, his right hand over his eyes, and his left holding a lantern which emitted a pale yellow glow, beneath which his face was almost as wan and white as his bleached hair.

He looked at me anxiously, questioningly, I thought. Instinctively, I inquired if Mr. Fanshawe were unwell.

"Are you a doctor?" he asked, almost in a whisper; adding, on my reply in the negative, "I hoped you might be. I fear the master is dying."

Startled, I unburdened myself of my wet overcoat, and then followed the man along a rambling passage. On the way, he confided to me that though Mr. Fanshawe was up and about, he had been very strange of late, and that he ate little, slept little, and was sometimes away on the Moss or the higher moors for ten or twelve hours at a time; further, that within the last few days he had become steadily worse.

Even this forewarning did not adequately prepare me for the change in my friend. When I saw him, he was sitting in the twilight before a peat fire on which a log, aflame at one end though all charred at the other, burned brightly. His hair was quite white: so white that that of his man, Robert Hoare, was of a yellow hue by comparison. It hung long and lank about his cadaverous face, which, in its wanness and rigid lines, was that of a corpse, except for the dark luminous eyes I remembered so well, once more like what they were in the days I first knew him, but now so intensely, passionately alive, that it was as though the flame of his life were concentred there. He rose, stiffly and as though with difficulty, and I saw how wofully thin he had become. It was with a shock of surprise I realized what vitality the man still had, when he took my hand in his, gripped it almost as powerfully as of yore, and half led, half pushed me into an arm-chair opposite his own.

Yes, he admitted, he had been ill, but was now better. Soon, he hoped, he would be quite well again. The eyes contradicted the lie of the lips.

After a time, our constraint wore off; but though I avoided the subject of his health and recent way of life, he interrupted me again and again to assure me that he would not have let me come so far, to visit so dreary a house, and see so unentertaining an invalid, had he known how to intercept me.

Suddenly he rose, and insisted on showing me over the house. Room by room fascinated me; but that small chamber of which I have already spoken, that with the crucifix, gave me nothing short of an uncontrollable repugnance, something akin to horror. He noticed this, though neither the lips offered nor the eyes invited any remark.

No wonder that from the several ominous circumstances of this meeting I was half prepared for some unpleasant or even tragic *dénouement*. But, as a matter of fact, nothing happened to alarm or further perturb me; and long before I went to my room I had noticed a marked improvement in Fanshawe, — that is, in his mental condition; physically, he was still very distraught as well as frail, and appeared to suffer extremely from what I took to be nervous cold, though he said it was the swamp-ague. "The Moss Fiend had got him," he declared. He wore a long frieze overcoat, even as he sat by the fire; and all the time, even at our frugal supper, kept his hands half covered in thick mittens.

Naturally enough, I did not sleep for long. In the first place, sleep is always tardy with me in absolutely windless or close, rainy weather; then the absolute silence, the sense of isolation, affected me; and, more effectually still, I could hear Fanshawe monotonously walking to and fro in the room to my right. This room, moreover, was no other than the fantastically decorated ante-chamber. I could scarce bear to think of my distraught friend, sleepless, and wearily active, in the company of that terrifying crucifix, that chamber of the myriad reduplications of the Passion. But at last I slept, and slept well; nor did I wake till the late sunlight streamed in upon me through the unshuttered and blindless window.

We spent most of that day in the open air. The morning was so blithe and sweet, Fanshawe lost something of his air of tragic ill; and I began to entertain hopes of his ultimate recovery. But in the early afternoon, when we had returned for the meal which had been prepared for us an hour before, the weather changed. It grew sultry and overclouded. The glass, too, had fallen abruptly. The change affected my friend in a marked degree. He became less and less communicative, and at last morose and almost sullen.

I proposed another walk. He agreed, with an eagerness that surprised me. "I will show you one or two places where I often go," he added: "places that the country people about here avoid; for the moor-folk are superstitious, as all who live in remote places are."

The day, as I have said, had become dull and heavy; and what with the atmospheric change, and the saturnine mood of my companion, I felt depressed. The two gaunt chimneys which rose above their respective mines were my skeletons at the feast. Otherwise I could have enjoyed many things in, and aspects of, that unfamiliar country; but these tall, sombre, bat-haunted, wind-gnawed "stacks," rising from dishevelled ruins, which, again, overlay the deserted lead-mines, oppressed me beyond all reason.

At one of these we stopped. Fanshawe asked me to throw something into a hollow place beyond one of the walls of a building. I lifted a large stone, and threw it as directed. I thought, at first, it had fallen on soft grass, or among weeds and nettles, for no sound was audible. Then, as it were underfoot, I heard a confused clamour, followed by the faint echo of a splash.

"That will give you some idea of the depth of the mine," my companion remarked quietly. "But it is deeper than you imagine, even now. There are sloping ledges *under* that water in which the stone fell at last; and beneath these ledges are corridors leading far into the caverns whence nothing ever comes again."

"It is not a place for a nervous person to come to," I answered, with as much indifference as I could assume; "nor for any one after sundown, and alone."

Fanshawe looked at me passively, then said quietly that he often came there.

"I wonder," he added, "how many dead will arise from a place like this when the trump of the Resurrection stirs the land?"

"Has anyone ever fallen into this mine, or been murdered in it?"

"They say so. It is very likely. But come: I will show you a stranger thing."

So on we trudged again, for, I should think, nearly a mile, and mostly through a thin wood. I wondered what new unpleasant feature of this unattractive country I was to see. It was with half angry surprise I was confronted at last by a thick scrub of gorse, overhung by three large birches, and told that there was what we had come to see. Naturally, there was nothing to arrest my attention. When I said so, however, Fanshawe made no reply. I saw that he was powerfully affected, though whether grief or some other emotion wrought him, I could not determine.

Suddenly he turned, said harshly that he was dead tired, and wished to go home straightway. Beyond a statement about a short cut by Dallaway Moor, he did not vouchsafe another remark until we reached the Manor.

At the entrance, Hoare met us, and was about

to speak, when he saw that his master was not listening, but rigid, with moving jaw, and wild eyes, was staring at the panels of the door.

"Who . . . who has been here?" he cried hoarsely; but for answer the man merely shook his head stupidly, muttering at last that not a soul had been near the place.

"Who has been here? Who has been here? Who did this?" my friend gaspingly reiterated, as he pointed to a small green cross, the paint still wet, impressed a foot or more above the latch.

III.

FANSHAWE was taciturn throughout the first part of the evening. We ate our meal in silence. Afterwards, in his study, he maintained the same self-absorption, and for a long time seemed unaware that he was not alone. The atmospherical oppression made this silence still more obvious. Even the fire burned dully, and the smoke that went up from the mist-wet logs was thick and heavy.

It was with a sense of relief I heard an abrupt, hollow, booming sound, as of distant guns at sea. The long-expected thunder was drawing near. For many minutes after this, the silence could be heard. Then there came a blast of wind that struck the house heavily, for all the world like an enormous billow flooding down upon and all but engulfing a dismasted ship.

Fanshawe raised his head, and listened intently. A distant, remotely thin wail was audible for a few seconds: the voice of the wind-eddy far away upon the moors. Then, once more, the same ominous silence.

"I hope the storm will break soon," I said at last.

"Yes. We'll have one or two more blasts like that, then a swift rain; then the night will become black as ink, and the thunderstorm will rage for an hour or so, and suddenly come back upon us again worse than before."

I looked at my friend surprisedly.

"How can you tell?"

"I have seen many thunderstorms and gales on these moorlands."

I was about to say something further, when I saw a look upon my companion's face which I took to be that of arrested thought or arrested speech.

I was right in my surmise, for, in a low voice, he resumed:—

"You will doubtless hear many another storm such as this. As for me, it is the last to which I shall ever listen: unless, as may well be, the dead hear. After all, what grander death-hymn could one have?"

"You are ill, Fanshawe, but not so ill as you believe. In any case, you do not fear you are going to die to-night?"

He looked at me long and earnestly before he answered.

"I — suppose — not," he said slowly, at last, but in the meditative way of one revolving a dubious matter in his mind: "no, I suppose not necessarily *to-night.*"

A long discordant cry of the wind came wailing across the Reach o' Dallaway. It was scarce gone, when a ponderous distant crashing betokened the onset of the elemental strife to be fought out overhead.

The effect upon Fanshawe was electric. He rose, moved to and fro, twice went to the window, and drew up the blind. The second time, he opened the latch. The window was of the kind called half-French; that is, it was of a single sheet of glass, but came no further than two thirds of the way down, the lower third being of solid wood, and could be opened (drawn inward) only in its glazed section.

He withdrew the fastening, stooped, and peered into the yard. A stealthy, shuffling sound was audible, followed by a low whine.

Fanshawe seemed satisfied, and, having closed the latch, drew together the thick, heavy curtains.

"That was my bloodhound, Grailph," he explained. "I always let him out at night. He keeps watch here. He is a huge beast, cream-white in color, and so is as rare and remarkable as he is trustworthy. I brought him, as a puppy, from Transylvania. The people hereabouts hate and fear him: the more so, because of his name. I have told you about the legend of Grailph Moss? Yes? Well, the rumour has filtered from mind to mind that my Grailph is no other than the original Grailph, or Grey Wolf; and that in some way he, I, and the 'House o' Fanshawe' are connected in an uncanny destiny."

"Are you quite sure you're not?" I interrupted, half in badinage, half in earnest.

He took my remark seriously, however.

"No; I am *not* sure. But who can tell what is the secret thing that lies hidden in the ninth shadow, the ninth wave, and the brain of a ninth child?"

"Ah, you remember what old Mark Zengro said that day by the cavern of the Jällusietch, in Bohemia! How well I remember that afternoon: how he called you Brother, and . . ."

"Well?"

"Oh, and what a strange talk we had afterwards by the fire, when . . ."

"No; that was not what you were going to say. You were about to add: '*How angry you were when Zengro made with his forefinger the sign of a circle about him; and how you nearly left the camp then and there.*' Is not that true?"

"Yes, it is true."

"I thought so. Well, I had good reason to be angry."

"Oh, his action meant only that he took you to be fëy, as we say in the north."

"No, it meant more than that. But this brings me to what I have wanted to say to you: what must be told to-night."

He stopped, for the roar about the house shook it to its foundations: one of those swift, howling whirlwinds which sometimes precede the steady march of the mighty host of the thunder.

When it was over, he pulled away the smoking logs from the fire and substituted three or four of dry pine and larch, already dusted with salt. The flame was so vivid and cheerful that, when my host eclipsed the lamplight, and left us in the pleasant firelit gloom, the change was welcome, though the wildness of the night without seemed to be enhanced.

For at least five minutes Fanshawe sat silent, staring into the red glow over which the blue and yellow tongues of flame wove an endless weft. Then, abruptly, he began:[1]—

"You know that I have Gypsy blood in me. It is true. But I do not think you know how strong in the present, how remote in the past, the strain is. In the twelfth century my parental ancestors were of what might be called the blood-royal among the Children of the Wind. One of them, head of a great clan at that time dispersed, during the summer months, through the region of the New Forest, was named John the Heron. Hunting one day in these woodlands, the king's brother was set

---

[1] His narrative, in its earlier stages, was much longer than my partial reproduction of it; for some of it dealt with irrelative matters, some of it was merely reminiscent of our own meetings and experiences in common, and some of it was abruptly discursive. Interwrought with it were the sudden tumults, the tempestuous violence of that night of storm: when, through it all, the thunder was to me as the flying shuttle in the Loom of Destiny.

upon by outlaws. They would have killed, or at least withheld him against a ransom, but for the bravery of his unknown gypsy ally. The royal duke was grateful, and so in turn was the king. Wild John the Heron became John Heron of Roehurst and the lands round Elvwick. He had seven sons, five of whom died tragic deaths or mysteriously disappeared. The eldest in due time succeeded his father; the youngest travelled into Derbyshire in the train of a great lord. In those days the most ancient, the proudest, but even then the most impoverished of the old families of that region, was the house of Ravenshawe. Its head was Sir Alurëd Ravenshawe, a man so haughty that it was said he thought the king his inferior. Gilbert Heron was able to do him a great service; and ultimately, through this influence, the young man succeeded to the name and titles of a beggared and outlawed knight, Sir Vane Fanshawe. Nevertheless, there could have been no question of the marriage of the young Sir Gilbert Fanshawe (for the name of Heron was to be relinquished) with the lady Frida, though the young people had fallen in love with each other at their first meeting; and, ultimately, it was permitted at all, and then reluctantly, only because of two further happenings. The first of these was the undertaking of the great lord with whom the young man was (a nearkins man and friend of Sir Alurëd Ravenshawe), that the king would speedily make Sir Gilbert Fanshawe of Roehurst in Hants and Eastrigg in the shire of Derby, a baron. At that time, there was no actual village of Eastrigg, but only a small hamlet called Fanshawe, or, as it was then given, The Fan Shawe. These lands belonged to Ravenshawe, and he gave them to his daughter as a wedding gift, on the condition that the king made her betrothed a noble, and that he became known as Baron Fanshawe of Fanshawe.

"All this was duly done, and yet there seems to have been deception in the matter of the Gypsy origin; for about the time of the birth of an heir to my lord of Fanshawe, Sir Alurëd refused to hold any communication with his son-in-law, or even to see his daughter. A Ravenshawe, he declared, could have nothing in common with a base-born alien.

"It was some years after this that strange rumors got about concerning not only Lord

Fanshawe but also The Chase, as his castellated manor was called. A wild and barbaric folk sojourned in its neighbourhood, or in the adjacent forests. A contagion of suspicion, of a vague dread, of a genuine animosity, spread abroad. Then it was commonly averred that my lord was mad, for had he not been heard to proclaim himself the Christ, or at any rate to speak and act as though he were no other than at least the second Christ, of whose coming men dreamed?

"One day Sir Alurëd Ravenshawe appeared in the camp of the Egyptians, as the alien wandering-folk were wont to be called. What he learned from the patriarch infuriated him to frenzy. 'Let the dog of the race of Kundry die the death he mocks,' he cried; 'and lo, herewith I give you my bond that no harm shall come to you or your people's goods, though you must sojourn here no more.'

"Then it was that the Egyptians waylaid their kinsman, the Lord Fanshawe of Fanshawe, and crowned and mocked him as the Gypsy Christ, and crucified him upon a great leafless tree in the forest now known as the Wood o' Wendray. Thereafter, for a long period, the place knew them no more. But, in going, they took secretly with them the infant Gabriel, only child of the House o' Fanshawe."

For a time after this, Fanshawe ceased speaking. We both sat, our gaze intent upon the fire, listening to the growing savagery of the storm without. Then, without preamble, he resumed. He had a habit, when in the least degree wrought by impatience or excitement, of clasping and unclasping his hands; and his doing so now was the more noticeable because of the strange tapery look of the fingers coming from the rough close mittens he wore.

"That Gabriel Fanshawe never saw England again, nor yet his son Gabriel. The name was retained privily, though among his blood-kin in Austria or Hungary he was known simply as Gabriel Zengro, the kin-name of the patriarch who had adopted him after the crucifixion of his father.

"Long before his grandson was a man well over forty years,—and it was not till then that the third Gabriel visited England to see if he could claim his heritage,—the lands of Eastrigg, the house and hamlet of Fanshawe, and Wester Dallaway, not only were exempted from all claim upon them by any one of the blood of Gilbert Fanshawe, the baronry in whose name was cancelled, but had, in turn, passed from the hands of the old knight of Ravenshawe into those of the family of Francis, with whom they remained until the fall of the Jacobite dynasty, after which they were held by the Hewsons, until (sadly diminished) they came again into the ownership of a Fanshawe, with my purchase of them.

"But though Gabriel Zengro the third found that he had lost his title and northern inheritance, he was able to recover possession of Roehurst. There he settled, married, and had two children: known only, of course, by his English surname. In the fiftieth year of his age he became markedly unpopular with his fellows. He was seen at times to frequent a rude and barbaric sect of vagrants,— even to live with them; and the rumour spread that his foreign wife was really one of these very aliens. Then he was heard to say wild and outrageous things, such as might well hang a man in those times. The upshot was that one day he returned to his home no more. His body was found transfixed to a leafless tree in the forest beyond Grailph Moss."

"Beyond Roehurst, you mean?" I interrupted.

"No, I mean what I say. His crucified body was found in the forest beyond Grailph Moss, in that part of it called The Wood o' Wendray."

"That is," I interrupted again, "where the same frightful tragedy had been enacted in the instance of the victim's grandfather?"

"Even so. But though Gabriel Fanshawe had been lured or persuaded or kidnapped out of Hants, he was certainly alive after he crossed the Derwent, for a huntsman recognised him among his people one day, and spat on the ground to the north, south, east, and west. The lord of Roehurst disappeared in this mysterious fashion; and none of his neighbours of the south learned aught of his doom, but only his wife knew, the tidings having been conveyed to her I know not how. But from the record she put in writing, it is clear that with the message had come a summons, perhaps a menace; for, together with her two children, she betook herself to the greater safety of London. There the girl died, calling vainly, and uttering strange words in a tongue no one spake or understood. But the boy lived, and in course of years grew to manhood, and on the death of his mother went to reside upon his own lands. Nor was it till after his marriage, and the birth of a son, that he read the record his mother had caused to be writ; and so came into the knowledge that has been the awe and terror of those lineally descended from him.

"But neither he nor his son came to any harm, save the common doom of all. Of his grandson wild things were said, but all that is known certainly is that he hanged himself upon the great oak in front of Roehurst. He too, however, had left a Gabriel behind him as his successor: in due time a good knight and learned man, who brought up his only child worthily and steadfastly. Strange that the heir of two such loyal and excellent men should prove so feather-brained as to love the woods better than the streets, and the wild people of the woods better than courtiers and scholars! Stranger still that the old omens should recur, till, at last, Gervase Fanshawe, after an awful curse upon all of his blood, and terrifying blasphemies, openly set fire to his manor; and himself, with his little daughter (though the young Gabriel escaped), was consumed in the flames.

"Thus, with tragic alternations, went the lives

of my forbears; till, after many generations of English Fanshawes, the house of Roehurst came to an end with Jasper Fanshawe."

At that moment so savage an onslaught of wind and rain was made upon the house, so violent a quake of thunder shook the walls, that further speech was impossible for the time. But, save by his silence, my companion took no notice of the tumult. His eyes were very large and wild, and stared spell-bound upon the fire, as though they beheld there the tragic issues to the many memories or thoughts which tyrannised his brain.

"I said that the family of Roehurst," he resumed, as soon as comparative quietude had followed that wild outburst, though the wind moaned and screamed round the gables and among the old chimneys, and the rain slashed against the window-pane in continuous assault,— "I said that the family of Roehurst came to an end with Jasper Fanshawe. This was at the close of the eighteenth century. Jasper was the last of his race, and, the rumour ran, one of the wildest. Almost on the eve of his wedding it transpired, that when, in his youth, he had gone away with and lived among the gypsy-people, he had, as most if not all of his progenitors, married a Romany girl. The union was not one that would be recognised by the English law; but the authentic news of it, and the confirmed rumour that Squire Fanshawe had a son and daughter living, brought about a duel between him and the brother of his betrothed. With rash folly this duel was fought in the woods, and witnessed by no one save the gypsy 'messenger' who kept the squire always in view."

"The gypsy-messenger, Fanshawe?"

"Yes. That is the name sometimes used. The old word means the doom-watcher. The latter is the better designation, but I did not care to use it.

"Well, my ancestor killed the man Charles Norton. The deed was the worse for the survivor, in that Norton was the favorite son of the most influential man in the country-side. In a word, the slaying was called murder, and Jasper Fanshawe was proclaimed. His sole chance lay with his blood-folk. The doom-watcher came into Winchester, and testified to what he had seen, while hiding among the bracken in the forest; but his evidence was overborne, and, rightly or wrongly, he was himself clapped into prison on a charge of rick-burning.

"No trace could be found of the fugitive, nor of the 'Egyptians' with whom he made good his escape. The large encampment in Elvwick Wood had broken up into sections, which had severally dispersed, and all had vanished almost as swiftly and effectually as the smoke of the camp-fires.

"Whatever I may surmise, I do not know for certain the manner of Jasper Fanshawe's death. His son, James, lived for the most part in Hungary; at other times in the wide-roaming lands between the Caspian and the Adriatic. He took in preference the old kin-name of Herne, which, indeed, his father had adopted after his flight from England.

"This James Herne lived to an old age, and became one of the 'elder brothers' of his particular tribal branch. His son Gabriel, however, left his kindred, and went to Vienna, where he studied medicine. Then, while still relatively a young man, he gained an important post at Prague, and in a year or so became what would here be called a magistrate. He was noted for his severity in dealing with all vagrants, but especially in the instance of any gypsy delinquent. At this time, as from his early Vienna days, he was known as Vansar, a Romany equivalent for Fanshawe. On three separate occasions, his life was attempted, though each time the would-be assassin escaped. Gabriel Vansar was not the man to be intimidated; indeed, he became only the more stringent and tyrannical, so that soon there was not a gypsy encampment within a twenty-mile radius of Prague. In his thirty-sixth year he was offered a medical professorship in Vienna. In that city he met a Miss Winstane, a beautiful English girl, the sole child of Edward Winstane, a Justice of the Peace for South Hants, and Squire of Roehurst Park and the greater part of the Parish of Elvwick. Miss Winstane loved her handsome wooer, and the marriage was duly solemnised. Though he spoke with a slight foreign accent, Mr. Vansar knew his paternal language thoroughly; for though 'James Herne' had ceased to be English in all else, he had been careful to teach his son his native tongue, and indeed always to speak it when alone with him.

"Neither Mr. Winstane nor Winifred Winstane ever knew that Gabriel Vansar was Gabriel Herne the Gypsy, or, in turn, that he was the grandson of that Jasper Fanshawe whose flight from Roehurst had been followed by the confiscation of his property, and its disposal to Edward Winstane the elder.

"As a matter of fact, Mr. Winstane died a few months after the marriage of his daughter. Gabriel Vansar now relinquished his post, and went to England to live the life of a country squire. There he had three children born to him: two sons and a daughter. Naomi was the youngest by several years, and at her coming her mother went. Of the two sons, Jasper was the elder, I the younger."

IV.

Although not taken wholly by surprise, I exclaimed, "*You*, Fanshawe?"—adding that indeed the chain of circumstances was remarkable.

"Yes. . . . Well, when my brother was twenty-one, and I nineteen, our father died. He had changed much since our mother's decease, and had become strangely depressed and even morose. There was adequate explanation of this in the sealed papers which he left to Jasper.

"But now I must diverge for a moment. I have something very strange to confide to you. . . . But first tell me: have you heard of Kundry?"

"Of Kundry?" I repeated, bewildered.

"You love music, I know; and I thought you might have heard of Kundry."

"Ah, yes, I know now. You mean the woman in Parsifal?"

"Yes. At the same time, Wagner does not give the true legend. He did not even know that the name is a gypsy one, and very ancient. I have heard that some people think it imaginary; others, that it is old-time Scandinavian. But our people, the Children of the Wind, are far more ancient than any one knows. We had earned that very name long before the Coming of the Christ. We had, however, another name, which were I to translate literally, would be something like 'The Spawn of Sheitan:' given us because we were godless, and without belief in any after-life, and were kingless and homeless and, compared with other peoples, lawless. As we were then, so in a sense we are now: for though we do not deny God, we neither worship him nor propitiate him nor fear him; nor have we any faith in a future, believing that with the death of the body that which is the man is dead also; and kingless we are, save for the common overlords, Time and Death; and homeless, except for the curtains of the forest and the dome of the sky, and the lamps of sun and moon; and, even as the wind is lawless and the sea, so also are we, who are more unstable than the one and more vagrant than the other.

"Nearly nineteen hundred years ago a tribe of our race, 'the first tribe' it was called, because it claimed to be the original stock, was in the hill-country beyond Jerusalem.

"It was in the year of the greatest moment to the modern world: the year of the death of Jesus of Nazareth.

"I need not repeat even in the briefest way details which are universally familiar. It is enough to say that some of our people were on the Hill of Calvary on the Day of Anguish; that among them was a beautiful wanton called Kundry; and that as the Sufferer passed to His martyrdom, she laughed in bitter mockery. Turning upon her, and knowing the darkness of her unbelief and the evil of which she was the embodiment, the Christ stopped and looked at her.

"'Hail, O King!' she laughed mockingly. 'Vouchsafe to me, thy Sister, a sign that thou art indeed Lord over Fate; but thou knowest thou canst not do this thing, and goest to thy death!'

"Then the Christ spake. 'Verily, thou shalt

have a sign. To thee and thine I bequeath the signs of my Passion, to be a shame and horror among thy people, forevermore.'

"Therewith He resumed His weary way. And Kundry laughed, and followed. Again, during the Agony on the Cross, she laughed, and again at the last bitter cry of the Son of God; but in the darkness that suddenly came upon the land she laughed no more.

"From that day the woman Kundry, whom some have held to be the sister of the Christ, was accurst. Even among her own people she went veiled. Two children she bore to the man who had taken her to his tent: children of one birth, a male child and a woman child.

"They were in their seventh year, when, in a wild Asian land, Kundry came out among her people and told them that she, the Sister of Christ, had come to deliver them this message, that out of the offspring of her womb soon or late would arise one who would be their Redeemer, who would be the Gypsy Christ.

"When the young men and maidens of her people mocked, the elders reprimanded them, and asked Kundry to give some proof that she had not the sun-fever or the moon-madness, or other distemper of the mind. Whereupon the woman appalled them by showing upon her hands and feet the stigmata of the Crucifixion.

"But, after the first wonder, and even awe, a great horror and anger arose among the kindred. Three days they gave her within which to take back that which she had said, and to confess the trickery of which she had been guilty, or at least to reveal the way in which she had mutilated herself and so healed the wounds. At sundown, on the third day, the strange and awful signs were still there; nor would the woman retract that which she had said. So they scourged her with thorny switches, and put a rough crown of them round her head, and led her to a place in the forest where there was a blasted tree. And as she went she stopped once, and looked to see whose mocking laugh made her last hour so bitter; and lo, it was the girl whom she had borne in her womb. Then they crucified her, and she gave up the ghost in the third hour before the dawn. But because that the children were so young, and bore no mark of the Curse, and were of the First Lineage, they were spared."

At this point my companion ceased. Leaning forward, he stared into the fire as one in a vision. A long silence prevailed. Outside, the wind wailed wearily, rising at times into a screaming violence. The heavy belching roar of the thunder crashed upon us ever and again, and even in the firelit room with its closed curtains the lightning-glare smote the eyes.

Fanshawe apparently did not hear; perhaps he did not see. I watched him intently, the more curiously because of what he told me and what I inferred. At last a strange, a terrifying cry startled even his abstraction. He sprang to his feet, and looked wildly at the window.

"It was the wind," I said; "I heard it like that a little ago, though not so loudly, or with so weird a scream."

Fanshawe made no reply. After a prolonged stare at the curtained window, and a nervous twisting and untwisting of his fingers, he seated himself again. Then, almost as though he had not broken his narration, he resumed:—

"The son and daughter of Kundry were spared by the enemies of the tribe as well as by their kindred, — or rather they escaped the cruelty of the one as well as the fanaticism of the other; for the tribe was almost exterminated by the shores of the Euphrates, and only Michael and Olah, the son and daughter of Kundry, with a few fellow-fugitives, reached a section of their race temporarily settled some fifty miles to the north.

"There 'the laughing girl,' as Olah was called, partly in memory of her mother, partly because of her own laughter at her mother's deathfaring, and partly because of the musical mockery wherewith she angered and delighted the tribesmen, brought unhappiness and ruin among 'the rulers.' There were three brothers of the ancient race, and each came to disaster and death through Olah. But through their death, Michael came to be what you would call the Prince of the Children of the Wind. There was but one evil deed recorded against him: the murder of his sister. But — so the ancient chronicle goes — this act was not out of cowardice or malice; it was to remove the curse of the mother, not only from those of her blood, but from the race. The deed was done in the year when Michael's wife bore him their second child, a girl. Before Olah's death, — and she died in the same way as her mother, — she took the little Sampa in her arms, and breathed her life into it. On the day of the crucifixion, the child turned in her sleep, in her mother's arms, and laughed as child never laughed before.

"The story thereafter is a long one. It is all in the secret record of our people, though known to a few only. I could tell it all to you, with every name and every happening, but this would serve no purpose to-night. Suffice it, that link by link the chain is unbroken from Michael and Sampa, the children of Michael, brother of Olah, the son and daughter of Kundry who laughed at the Christ on Calvary, even unto the three offspring of Gabriel Fanshawe, who was called Vansar, and was of the tribe of the Heron."

Could it be, I wondered, as I looked intently at the speaker, that this man before me was the lineal descendant of that Kundry who had laughed at Christ; that he was the inheritor of the Curse; and that for him, perhaps, as for so many of his race, the ancestral doom was imminent? With an effort I conquered the superstitious awe which I realised had come upon me.

"Do you mean this thing," I said slowly, "do you mean that you, James Fanshawe, are the direct descendant of Kundry, and that the Curse lives, and that you or some one of your blood, whether of this or a later generation, must 'dree the weird' even as your forbears have done?"

"Even so: I am as I say; and the Curse lives; and no man can evade the doom that is nigh two thousand years old."

I waited a few minutes, pondering what best to say. Then I spoke.

"The story is a strange and terrible one, Fanshawe. But even if exactly as you have told it, surely there is no logical necessity why you or your brother or sister should inherit the Curse. There has, by your own admission, been frequent admixture of a foreign and Christian strain in your lineage. Your father was, to all practical intents, no more a gypsy than I am. He married an English girl, and lived the life of a country squire, and was no different from his kind except in his perhaps exaggerated bitterness against gypsies, — though, by the way, not as different in this respect either, for the country gentleman loveth not the vagrant. In a word, he himself, with all his knowledge of the past, would have laughed at your superstitious application of the legend."

Fanshawe turned upon me his great luminous eyes, aflame with the fire of despair. I could see that he was in passionate earnest.

"*My sister* might have laughed," he said in a voice so low as almost to be a whisper, but with significant emphasis: "*my sister* might have laughed, not my father."

"Why, Fanshawe," I exclaimed, startled, "you do not mean to say that your sister is — is — "

"A daughter of Kundry."

I received the remark in silence. I did not know what to think, much less what to say. My nerves, too, were affected by the electric air, the ever-recurrent surge and tumult of the thunderstorm; and I felt bewildered by what I heard, by what, despite its improbability, I knew that I believed. At last I asked him to resume, saying I knew he had not ended what he had set himself to tell me.

"No, I have not ended.

"From what I have told you, you will have gathered that the Curse does not show itself in every generation, but in the third. I cannot say that the death record is unvarying, for I do not know; nor has it been possible to trace every particular of a remote ancestry. But here is a strange thing: that in all but three instances, so far as known, no son or daughter of Kundry has ever had more than two children. From generation to generation that bitter laugh has never lapsed. From generation to generation it has brought about disaster and shame. Many, even as I have done, have dreamed that the Curse might be expiated or outlived; but it may well be that even as in every generation 'the laughing girl' who is of the race of Kundry mocks God, so in every third generation, till the Christ come again or the world be no more, there may be the tragedy of my ancestral woe.

"All this, my father knew ere he died. He had meant to carry the secret to the grave, and by many precautions believed he had safeguarded his children from contact with the people he hated and dreaded, though he was of them himself.

"About the time when my father's morose and brooding manner was first noted, my brother Jasper had fallen ill. It was a mysterious trouble, and no doctor could name the malady. Once, only, I saw my father furious, — on the day when he learned that there was an encampment of gypsies in Elvwick Woods, and that Jasper, who was as impassioned in religion as Saint Francis himself, had been among the wandering people, striving to win them to the Brotherhood of Christ. Our father did not know that I and my sister Naomi had already discovered the camp, and had been fascinated by the dark people and their way of life and the forest freedom, — so that we could think of little else, and yearned to be in the greenwood, even as a bird to spread its wings beyond the bars of its cage.

"It must have been immediately after this that my father made the discovery which changed him from one man to another. Neither Naomi nor I knew aught of it at the time, though we were aware that something dire had happened, something of awe, of dread.

"For when Jasper rose from his bed of sickness there was upon his feet and upon his hands the purple bruise and ruddy cicatrix of the great nails of the Crucifixion."

For a few moments Fanshawe paused, and

drew a painful, labored breath, as of a man in pain or a great weakness.

"After our father's death, Jasper shut himself up in his room, and would see no one. I used to creep along the passage at dusk, and listen to the wild incoherences of his prayers. We, Naomi and I, were very dismal, and it was with relief when, one evening, we fled into the forest, and joined our friends, more mysterious and alluring than ever because of the terrifying things which had been said of them by him who was now dead.

"Our shortest way was by Elvwick churchyard. Perhaps but for this we would not have thought of looking at our father's grave again: for we did not mean to return to Roehurst. Hand in hand, however, we stole to the spot we had already ceased to regard with the first overwhelming awe.

"The shock was greater than even that of his death had been, for we saw that the grave had been rifled. The coffin was visible, but the lid had been forced open. There was no corpse within. Almost too dazed to be frightened, it was some time before I realised that the outrage must have been committed that very night;

for the upturned earth had retained its fresh smell, an axe was lying near the grave, and there were imprints of feet in the damp soil.

"The idea flashed across my mind that our father had somehow come to life again,—perhaps, I thought, he knew of our intended flight and had gone back to Roehurst to frustrate it,—and I could scarce move with terror. Naomi laughed, a strange mirthless laugh that made me turn as though to strike her. Then, shivering and sobbing, we crawled away. I think we were about to return home, when a tall figure arose, called us by our names, and invited us to come and see the merry 'Dance of the Wolves' around the camp-fire. I told the man—Mat Lee, I remember his name was—what had happened. To my surprise he did not appear shocked or frightened. He was silent for a little; then in a whisper he urged us to run with him at once, lest we should meet the dead man on his way back from the house to the grave.

"That is how my sister and I went to live among our unknown kindred. The very next day, at dawn, the camp was lifted; a week thence we were in Brittany. It was not till long afterwards I learned that it was the tribesmen who had desecrated my father's grave. 'He had been a renegade, and the enemy of his race,' they said, 'and it was only right that though he had lived in honor he should afterwards be flung back to earth as a dead dog is hurled among the bramble or gorse.'

"Once, only, I saw my brother again. I know that he did his best for us. He traced our flight, and kept in touch with us. A 'commando' was sent to him, forbidding him to come near us, or even to go among his kindred anywhere. I was told I was free to go and come as I liked, and that I had money always at my command. Naomi, however, had to abide with the tribe. For three years I roamed throughout the lands east of Saxony and Bavaria, and as far south as Dalmatia and Roumania. I had been well educated, and was a student; and I learned much, though in my own desultory fashion.

"Then tidings reached me that Jasper had disappeared. It was said that he had been seen in the shore-woods of Lymington, on the Solent; and that he had been drowned, while bathing or boating. An upturned boat had been discovered, in which he had certainly been that forenoon, for he had come in it from Yarmouth in the Isle of Wight.

"I went to England, and in due time entered into possession of the family property. At first (and this was when we met in Surrey), I thought of settling there, for a time. At last, however, I decided to dispose of Roehurst, and realise everything that had come to me; and I had done this, and was about to leave for eastern Europe when a letter reached me from Derbyshire. *It was in my brother's handwriting.*

"Bewildered, distraught, and angry, I read this strange and unlooked-for communication. The writer was alive, and begged me to come and save him from the enmity of the kindred with whom he had at the end cast in his lot. To narrate briefly what might well be told with lengthy and surprising detail, I reached Sheffield, and thence set out across the wild and remote country (to me at that time quite unknown, even by repute) which lies to the north of Dallaway Moor and Grailph Moss. At the verge of the great forest I was met by a gypsy guide. Late that night we reached the camp. From an hour after my arrival till the last hour of the night I was alone with my brother. He told me all that I have told you, and much else beside; also where his own and our father's papers were to be found. Finally, he declared that the Curse died with himself. He had had this revealed to him in a vision; besides, other circumstances, with which I need not weary you, pointed to this end. He had sworn this to the tribesmen, and they had consented to forego the manner of his death, if he would further renounce all claim to be the Gypsy Christ. The very name gave them a sense of horror and anger; his fervent words of exhortation had made them sullen, and at last resentful; and, over and above this, there was the vague race-legend that, whenever the Gypsy Christ should come, the days of the Children of the Wind would be numbered, and they would dwindle away like the leaves in October.

"An hour before dawn, three of the kindred entered the tent. They put a bandage about my eyes, and secured my arms. I heard them lift Jasper, and put him upon a hurdle of larch-boughs. In the chill air we went silently forth. In about a quarter of an hour we came to a standstill upon a rising ground. I heard Jasper repeat in a husky voice that he was not worthy to be the Christ; that he was not the Christ; and that he prayed that with him might pass away forever the curse of Kundry.

"There was a brief silence after that; then a rustling sound in the air; then, after an interval, a thud, thud, thudding, followed by a splash.

"'No man ever comes back from the bowels of the lead-mine, O James, of the tribe of the Heron, of the race of Kundry,' whispered a voice in my ear.

"When, an hour later, the bandage was taken from my eyes, I was on the moor just above the House o' Fanshawe. A boy was beside me, his face covered with a slouch hat. In a few words, in our ancient language, he told me that I was by the village of Eastrigg, and that twenty miles south of me lay Fothering Dale, whence I could easily go in any direction; anywhere, he added significantly, where the tongue can be silent and the memory dead.

"I made no inquiries about the matter I have told you. Fortunately I had informed no one of the letter I had received. This letter I burned. But I ran a great risk by returning a few days later to Eastrigg. The reason was this: I had learned, from the papers to which my brother had alluded, the whole story of our doomed race, the race of Kundry; and I decided to try one more desperate hazard against Fate, for I could not be sure that Jasper's death would remove the Curse. In a word, I decided to make my home in this place where my ancestor and brother suffered such cruel deaths, and to die here; for I found in my papers an ancient prophecy, both in English and Romany, to the effect that when a woman of the race of Kundry would voluntarily sacrifice herself at the Hill of Calvary, or when a man of the race of Kundry would live and die at the place where one of his kindred had suffered for the Curse, the doom might be removed.

"Thus it was that I became possessor of this strange 'House o' Fanshawe.' But I had something to do before I settled here.

"When everything that had to be done was done, I went abroad to seek my kindred, and more particularly my sister Naomi. Perhaps you guess my object. I had more hope of success, from the circumstance that Naomi was of a passionately enthusiastic nature; and that, of late, she had even dreamed of leaving her people (for one strain in her fought against the other), to enter a Sisterhood of Mercy.

"But my people had gone, and the clues were already old and complicated. I went through Hungary, across Transylvania, hither and thither in Roumania, and from end to end in Dalmatia. Everywhere I was on their track, but the trail was confused. It was not till I had gained the Bavarian highlands that the conclusion was forced upon me I was being misled. This became a certainty after I had followed a sure trail through Suabia and so to the Lands of the Moselle. At Trèves, I was directed southward, and went blindly on a false track that led through southern France towards the Basque provinces; but at last, at a place in Provence called Aigues-Mortes, I met a life-brother (that is, one whose life had been saved when otherwise it would have been lost, and who has vowed his life-service to his saviour, whenever required), whom I put upon his oath. He told me that the Zengri, the Hernes, and two other tribes were not in southern Europe at all, but in England. I had hit upon the right trail between Heidelberg and the Mösel, but, when almost upon my people at Trèves, had been skilfully diverted. And the reason for this was the extraordinary ascendancy of my sister. My heart sank as I heard this tiding. I feared that the Curse had already shown itself; but, my informant assured me, I was wrong in this surmise. It was merely that Naomi had fascinated the tribes-folk, and, particularly since the death of the old Peter Zengro, had become practically a queen. Her word was law.

"Of course I could not tell the exact reason why she wished to evade me. Possibly she feared I might resent her ascendancy, and try to usurp her; possibly she had some reason to fear that the always latent enmity against any of the race of Kundry would be directed against me. As likely as not, she had several schemes to fulfil, all or even one of which might be frustrated by my appearance on the scene.

"Nevertheless, I decided to travel straight to England, and, as soon as practicable, gain an interview with Naomi.

"For some weeks after I reached this country I was again purposely misled. Yet from one thing and another I became more and more anxious to meet Naomi soon. Strange rumours were abroad. At Ringwood in the New Forest, I overheard some words by the camp-fire (when I was supposed to be asleep) which made my heart shrink.

"Once again I lost all clue. Then it was that I remembered Nathan Lee, — an intimate friend of yours as well as of mine, — who, because of his great love for his wife, had sworn never to leave the neighborhood of Glory Woods, where she was buried. I travelled with all speed to Dorking. From Lee I learned what I wanted to know. By a strange fatality, Naomi had made her headquarters in the Wood o' Wendray, beyond Eastrigg. But was it a blind fatality? That was what troubled and perturbed me. Why had she, why had our particular tribe, settled at the accursed spot where Jasper Fanshawe had met his fate!

"It was at this time that I met you in Glory Woods. The next day I was back in the village of Elvwick, and had arranged with Robert Hoare, the late gardener at Roehurst, and his wife, to come and keep house and generally look after me, at Eastrigg Manor.

"Almost every day after I was settled I rode over to the Wood o' Wendray; but the ban was upon me, and I was warned not to approach the camp. Thrice I set the ban at defiance, and strode into the camp, but on no occasion saw any sign of Naomi. This was the more strange, as, on the third time, I arrived at sunset, 'the hour of the smoke,' when the gypsies meet round the fire to talk and smoke and break their long day-fast. It was after this third visit I was formally warned that my next defiance of the ban would be my last. I knew this to be no idle threat. Thereafter I had to be more cautious. I no longer rode across the moor; but, either in the morning twilight or in the late afternoon, wandered here and there across the uplands: sometimes by the deserted lead-mines, sometimes by the green pool, sometimes even within the outskirts of the Wood o' Wendray.

"I met you in Glory Woods in the spring, and now it is autumn. It was exactly midway in this time that I learned a dreadful thing.

"One day a message came to me, in Naomi's writing, to be at the green pool beyond Dallaway mine at dawn on the morrow.

"I was there, of course. The morning was raw and misty. Even at the margin of the

Pool I could not see the further side. Suddenly, however, I heard whispered voices, and the trampling of feet. I called, and was at once answered. I was bidden not to stir from where I was. The voice was that of Naomi, but with a note in it I had never heard before.

"'Is that you, James Fanshawe, of the tribe of the Heron, of the race of Kundry?'

"'It is I, Naomi, daughter of Gabriel. It is I, your blood-brother.'

"'Then know this thing. She whom you wedded secretly, Sanpriella Zengro, is dead.'

"I gave a cry of pain. . . . I have not told you that, during my last year with my people, I loved Sanpriella, the daughter of Alexander Zengro, the brother of Peter Zengro, of the First Tribe. But Alexander Zengro feared and hated any of the race of Kundry; so we loved secretly. This was one reason why I was so eager to find my people again; for Naomi was not, as you may have supposed, my one quest. I knew that Sanpriella was with child, and I longed to make her my wife before all men.

"'Is it so?' I cried in a shaking voice, because of my sore pain; 'is it so, upon the oath of the crossed sticks and the hidden way?'

"'I say it. May tree fall on me, and water gain upon me, and the falling star light on me, if I speak not truth. Sanpriella is dead. She lies in the wood of Heiligenberg, beyond the Neckar. And now listen to the doom, thou son of Kundry.'

"My heart leapt at these ominous words, doubly ominous and strange coming from one of my own blood.

"'Unto Sanpriella were born twin children, a boy and a girl. The girl lives, though you shall never see her. She is in a far land from here, and the lines of her life are already known. The boy ... the boy is ... dead.

"'But know this thing, James my blood-brother. The doom of Kundry was upon him. His mother hid the thing, but after her death the Curse was visible. Upon his hands were the bruised wounds of the nails of the Crucifixion.'

"With a shuddering cry I sank to my knees. Wildly I prayed, implored Naomi to say it was not true; that it was hearsay; that some natural cause had been mistaken for this horrible mystery.

"'Therefore,' she resumed unmoved, 'the ban is upon you also. Take heed lest a worse thing befall you. It will be well if you leave this place where you live, and forever. Be a wanderer upon the face of the earth; it will be for you safer so: but avoid the trail of the Children of the Wind as you would the pestilence. And now —farewell!'

"'My child lives — my daughter lives!' I cried despairingly.

"There was a long silence. I called again and again, but met with no response. Thick as the mist was, I raced round the pool like a greyhound. There was no one near. I ran out upon the moor, but there I was like a derelict boat in wide ocean in a dense fog. I could see nothing, hear nothing. All that day the mist hung impermeable; all that day I abode where I was."

Once more a long silence fell upon Fanshawe. Outside, the shrieking of the wind was appalling. The rain slashed against the house as though all the sluices of the thunderstorm were concentred there. The thunder was no longer overhead, but a raucous blast — distinct from the blind, furious gale — moved to and fro like a beast of prey. I was overcome by the strange and terrible tale I had listened to. Then and there, to that wild accompaniment, it all seemed deadly true, and as inevitable as Destiny.

With an abrupt gesture, Fanshawe suddenly resumed: —

"On the eve of that day I walked swiftly across the moor. The sun was almost on the horizon as I reached the easter edge of Grailph Moss. Suddenly, I stopped as one changed into stone. Black against the sunset-light I saw a tall figure stand: with head thrown back, and arms wide outstretched from the sides. Was it a vision of the Christ? That was the thought which came to me. Then the figure disappeared, absorbed in the mist over Grailph Moss. I turned and went home. It was Naomi I had seen.

"The next evening I was in the same place, at the same hour.

"Again I saw Naomi, in that sunflame Crucifixion. Once more she disappeared, and across the Moss. I knew of no encampment there, but unquestionably she had moved swiftly westward.

"On the third afternoon I was there again,

earlier. This time I had with me my white bloodhound. We crouched in good hiding till Naomi passed. I made Grailph sniff her track. When the sun set, she disappeared as before. I held Grailph in leash, and followed swiftly. In less than an hour I came upon her. She was standing in a waste place, near the centre of a broken circle of tall slabs. These were the Druidic Stones, known almost to none save the most daring explorers of the Moss, for they are in a region beset with quagmires.

"She was speaking, with outstretched arms, as if in prayer. There was no one visible. She was, I saw, in a trance, or ecstasy.

"When, suddenly, she descried me, she leapt like a deer on to a narrow dry path beyond the stones. She would certainly have evaded me but for Grailph. The hound slid beyond like running water in a rapid. In less than a minute he had headed her off.

"When I came up with her, I expected either furious denunciation, or at least a summary command that I should return straightway. She did no more than look at me intently, however. She had already forgotten what had lain between us. She was possessed.

"'*Naomi*,' I said, simply.

"'I am Naomi, blessed among women.'

"I stared, perplexed.

"'Why do you follow me here to spy me out? Beware lest God strike thee for thy blasphemy.'

"'My blasphemy, Naomi?'

"'Even so. I come here to meet the Spirit of God.'

"'Tell me, my sister, is this true what I have heard: that you are with child?'

"Her eyes flamed upon me. But her voice was cold and quiet as she replied, —

"It is true. The Lord hath wrought upon me a miracle. I have immaculately conceived, and the child I shall bear will be the Gypsy Christ, — the long dreamed-of, the long waited-for second Christ.'

"'This is madness. Come with me; come home with me, Naomi.'

"'The green earth is my home; and the wind is my brother, and the dust my sister.'

"'Come!'

"Then in a moment her whole look and mien changed. The flame that was in her eyes seemed to come from her very body. Her voice now was loud, raucous, imperious. The hound whined, and sidled to my feet.

"'I am the Sister of Jesus, I am no other than Kundry, deathless in my woe until these last days. I am the Mother of the Christ that is to be. And you, *you*, son of my mother's womb, you are ordained to be my prophet! Go forth even now: go unto our people in the woods: declare, declare, declare, to them, to all, that the Gypsy Christ cometh at last!'

"I was shocked, terrified even. But after a throbbing silence, I spoke, and firmly, —

"'This is madness, Naomi. Already the Curse is heavy enough upon us. Do you not know that our brother Jasper was done to death yonder because of this doom of ours; that because of this awful malison on the race of Kundry' . . . that . . . my little son . . .

"'I know all,— what has been, what is, what shall be. Once more I ask you: will you be the prophet of the Gypsy Christ?'

"'No, never, so help me God!'

"'This is the fourth day of this Week of the Miracle. To-morrow thou hast; and the day after; and yet again, another day. Repent while there is yet time. But if thou dost not repent, thine end shall be as that of thy dog. An awful sign shall be with thee this very night; yet another shall be with thee on the morrow; and on the third thou shalt receive the message of the Cross. Then thou shalt waver no more, for whom all wavering is forever past. And now, begone!'

"Broken in spirit, I turned. When, a hundred yards thence, I looked back, there was no trace of Naomi anywhere.

"That night I had the first sign."

Here Fanshawe ceased for a moment, and wiped the cold sweat from his forehead with a hand tremulous as a reed. His voice had sunk into a dull monotony, to me dreadful.

"On the day following, I had the second sign. Drops of blood oozed from the red figure of the Christ that you have seen in my room. Then, you came. To-day I have had the message of the Cross. You saw it yourself: a green cross on the portal of the house.

"Then at last my terror overmastered me. Also, I yet hoped to prevail with Naomi. Thus it was that when I left you abruptly this afternoon, I rode across the moor, to the Wood o' Wendray. I reached the camp, but only the ashes of dead fires were there. Yet I know my people wait, and Naomi has my life on the hollow of her hand."

But here I broke in eagerly.

"Come, Fanshawe, come with me at once, the first thing to-morrow. You must not be here another day. It is madness for you to remain. Why, in another week you would persuade yourself that you too had inherited this so-called curse!"

"*Look!*" he shouted, springing to his feet, tearing the coverings from his hands, and holding forth the palms to me, rigid, testifying, appalling: "*Look! Look! Look!*"

And as I live I saw upon the hands the livid stigmata of the Passion!

With a cry, I repelled him. A great horror seized me. But the next moment a greater pity vanquished my weakness. He had already fallen. I took him in my arms, and laid him back on his chair.

James Fanshawe was dead.

For some minutes I stared, paralysed, upon the still face that had just been so wrought with a consuming frenzy. A deep awe came upon me. I crossed the room, threw back the window, and looked out. Grailph the hound was not there. Nor could he have been lurking near, for at that moment I saw a man glide swiftly across the yard, and disappear into the gloom.

The rain was over, the thunder rumbled far across the moors; the wind, too, had veered, and I heard it crying like a lost thing, in the deep ravine of the Gap.

I stayed quietly beside my friend, keeping vigil till the dawn. While it was still dark, I went again to the window, and looked out. On the moor I could hear two larks singing at a great altitude. Doubtless they had soared to meet the dawnlight.

I thought of Naomi, whose madness would surely bring upon her, and that soon, the awful ancestral doom. Yet of this I knew I should hear nothing. The Children of the Wind have a saying: The dog barks by day, and the fox by night; but the Gypsy never lets any one know whence he comes, where he is, or whither he goes.

Sometimes the horror of it all makes me long to look upon it as an evil dream. Has the dreadful Curse at last worked itself out? With a sudden terror, I remember at times that James Fanshawe had two children born to him. What of the girl? Did she, too, laugh, when her kindred led Naomi to her doom? Even now doth she move swift and sure towards that day when she shall go quick with child; when she or the child or the child's child shall arise and say, "Behold the Gypsy Christ is come at last!"

MADGE O' THE POOL.

Madge o' the Pool:

A Thames Etching.

―•―

WHEN the January fog hangs heavy upon London it comes down upon the Pool as though it were sluiced there like a drain, or as a mass of garbage shot over a declivity in a waste place. The Pool is not a lovely spot in winter, though it has a beauty of its own on the rare days when the sun shines in an unclouded frosty sky, or when a northwester comes down from the distant heights of Highgate and Hampstead, and slaps the incoming tide with short splashes of waves washed up by the downward current, till the whole reach of the Thames thereabouts is a jumble of blue and white and of gleaming if dirty grays and greens. On midwinter nights, too, when the moon has swung up out of the smoke, like a huge fire-balloon adrift from the Lambeth furnaces, and when the stars glint like javelin points, there is something worth seeing down there, where the forest of masts rises sheer and black, and where there is a constant cross-flash of red and green rays from innumerable bow-lamps and stern-windows and tipsy lanterns trailed awry through the rigging. A mile up stream, and it is wonderful what stillness prevails. There is, of course, the dull roar of omnibuses and cabs on the bridges, the muffled scraping sound of hundreds of persons moving rapidly afoot, and, from the banks, the tumult of indiscriminate voices and sounds of all kinds round and beyond the crank-crank of the cranes on the grain-wharves and the bashing of the brick and coal barges against the wooden piers. But upon the interspaces of the river, what comparative silence! A disjointed passenger-boat, with spelican funnel darting back to the perpendicular, shoots from under a bridge, and paddles swiftly down-stream like a frightened duck; a few moments, and it is out of sight, swallowed in the haze, or swung round a bend. A trio of barges, chained to each other like galley-slaves, passes up-stream, drawn by what looks like a huge bluebottle-fly. The bluebottle

A Thames Etching. 77

is a tug-boat, a "barge-bug" in river parlance; and as it flaps the water with a swift spanking smash of its screw, the current is churned into a yeast of foam that is like snow against the bows of the first barge, and thin as dirty steam when washed from the sternmost into a narrow vanishing wake. As likely as not, the bargees are silent, pipely contemplative, taciturn in view of always imminent need for palaver of a kind almost unique in the scope and vigour of its blasphemy. Perhaps, however, the boy at the caboose forward whistles the tune of "O were I sodger gay" or that perennial favourite which recounts the deeds of Jack Do and Bob Did n't in the too familiar groves of Pentonville; or the seedy man in shirt-sleeves, who walks the starboard plank with a pole and thinks he is busy, may yell a ragged joke to a comrade similarly employed on one of the other barges. Or even, and indeed very probably, the heavily cravated, dogskin-capped helmsman may suddenly be moved to a hoarse volley of words so saturated, dominated, upheld, overborne by the epithet "bloody," that the "coal-bunker" might almost be taken for a slaughter-house escaping in disguise. But even the barges slump up-stream out of sight before long: and then, how quiet the river is for a space! The wharf-rats are so fat that they make a stone-like splash when they plunge through the grain-dollops; but only a practised ear could recognise the sound in the rude sussurrus of the current, or "spot" the shrill squeaks, as of a drowning and despairing penny-whistle, when a batch of these "Thames-chickens" scurries in sudden flight down a granary-slide and goes flop into the quagmires of mud left uncovered by the ebb. But at the Pool there is never complete silence. Even if there be no wind, the curses of the Poolites (in at least twenty varieties of human lingo) would cause enough current of air to crease the river's dirty skin here and there into a grim smile.

Like the rest of the world, the Pool has its sociable seasons. Broadly there are two. The shorter might be called that of the concertina and open-air "flings;" the longer that of the riverine singing-dens and dancing-saloons. But the regular population has not much time for systematic gaiety, not even in the long summer nights: a bad season, in fact, when there is little business to be done and too much light to do it in. The stranger visiting the neighbourhood — that is to say the stranger who carries in his aspect too obvious credentials as to his respectability — might laugh at the idea of there being a Pool population at all, that is, of a permanent kind. He will find the saloons in the locality haunted by a motley gathering, where as a rule the ladies show no insular partiality in their acceptance of partners either in the dancing-shops or other dens of more or less repute, and where, without having had the advantages of an excellent training at a young ladies' academy, they seem quite at ease with gentlemen of foreign parts, coloured or otherwise, who talk no lingo but their own. It is, in fact, a cosmopolitan society. The civilisation of the west and the wisdom of the east meet constantly in the intercourse of the Irish dock-labourer and the Chinese "grubber;" and the coolie or Malay is as much at home as the Dutchman or Portugee.

There is a clan of which almost nothing is known. It is the people of the Pool. Ask the river-police, and they will tell you something of the "water-rats," though if your informant be candid he will add that he can't tell you much. Many unfortunate travellers have met members of the fraternity; for one of their favourite and most reputable pursuits is the ferrying at exorbitant prices (the inevitable purloining skilfully carried on at a certain stage is not charged for) of would-be voyagers by the Hamburg and Baltic steamers, when, on account of the tide, embarkation has to take place midstream. The Poolites haunt Irongate and Horsleydown stairs, and are given to resenting active interest in their vested rights. But their chief means of life is otherwise obtained. They are the vermin of the Thames, and they scour its surface by night with irreproachable industry and thoroughness. It would not be easy to describe what they do, particularly under cover of mist or fog; it is simplest to say that they will do *anything*, except speak to a "cat" or refuse a drink. A "cat," it may be observed, is the name applied to a member of the river-police; and as the "cats" are always worrying, even when not directly chasing the Poolites, or "rats," the result is incompatibility of temper.

Many of the Poolites haunt holes and corners in the neighbourhood of Horsleydown stairs. Some have their lair in old boats, or among rotten sheds or wood-piles; others are as homeless, as well as unpleasant and as fierce as dung-beetles. Among them there are "rats" of either sex who are practically never ashore, whose knowledge of London is confined to familiarity with the grim river-frontages, and whose sole concern in connection with "the great name of England" is a chronic uneasiness about her might and majesty in the guise of the police.

A score or so of Poolites are marked men. That is to say, either through length of experience in loafing and vagabondage, or owing to proved crime, their names are known to the "cats," and their persons occasionally wanted. An invincible modesty characterises the Poolite. He sees no distinction in public arrest, and the halo of a conviction does not allure him. In a word, he is a water-rat, and wishes to remain one.

The fact that he was so well-known, and could generally be easily found, was a chronic sore in the drink-besotted mind of old Dick Robins. He loathed this distinction, and could he have gained prolonged credit at any other gin-shop than that of his brother Bill he would have shifted his quarters. The fact that, as a younger man, twenty years earlier, when he was about thirty, — for age does not go by years in every part of the world — he had thrice served his term in jail, may have prejudiced him against any radical change in his way of life. On the second occasion he had appropriated in too conspicuous a fashion the contents of a lady's pocket, the wife of a sea-captain with whom he had found it difficult to come to an exorbitant arrangement; and for this very natural action he was condemned to three years' imprisonment, with atrocious and objectionable hard labour. He would have been embittered against the law to the end of his days, if he had not been so far mollified by the light sentence on his third "go," one of six weeks, — thus light, as the charge was only of having brutally kicked his wife up and down a barge and then into the half-frozen Thames. As she died of rheumatic fever, Mr. Robins could not legally, of course, be held accountable. For twenty years or more Dick Robins had found gin so pleasing a mistress that he had been unable to give any but the most nominal attention — it would be absurd to say to the education — to the growth of his daughter. Her name was "girl:" that is, his name for her. Baptised Margaret, she was commonly called Madge. He realised that she was a girl, and comely, on account of various ideas of his own and suggestions from outside, all on the same level of profound depravity. He first regarded her as a woman when, having lost eleven and fourpence at Wapping-euchre to Ned Bull, that gentleman generously offered to overlook the debt, and to spend the remaining eight and eightpence of the broken quid in two bottles of "Jamaicy" and four goes of "Aunt Maria," conditionally on receipt of Madge as the legal Mrs. Bull. The offer would have been accepted right off, but Mr. Robins found to his chagrin that the bottles of rum and goes of proof-gin would not be consumable till the marriage festival.

Madge was a dark, handsome girl, tall, well-made though too thin, somewhat slatternly in dress, though generally with a clean face, and, stranger to say, with fairly clean hands. Neither she nor anyone else would have dreamed of the application to her of the term "beautiful." Only those who caught a glimpse of her as she stood in a statuesque pose, pole in hand, on some hay barge or hoy in ballast, or as she sculled up stream or down, deft as a duck in the fentangle, noticed the beauty of her thick-clustered, ample hair, and mayhap the splendour of her large, dark, velvety eyes. Madge knew very little of shore-life, even that of the Horsleydown neighbourhood, and nothing at all of the larger life of that vast metropolis which represented the world to her: though she was vaguely aware that beyond the Isle of Dogs the Thames widened to that sea which bore the foreign ships that came to London, and brought so many mariners of divers nationalities, all equally eager for two things: strong drink and purchaseable women. When ashore, she was generally at the house of her uncle Bill the publican, or, more often, at that of her sister-in-law, Nell Robins. For all her rough life, her rude imaginings, her uncouth surroundings, her ignorance of refinement in speech or manner, Madge was pure of heart, honourable in all her intimate dealings, and as upright generally as she had any call to be.

Dick Robins was coarse and brutal enough in his talk when she had refused to desert the river-life of the Pool in order to act as bar-maid at her uncle's public-house, the "Jolly Rovers." With all her experience, and she could have given points to most specialists in blasphemy, she learned the full vocabulary of utter degradation when she told her father that "Gawd hisself couldn't swop her to that beast, Ned Bull, without her will, which would never be till she was drownded, and not then."

The drink-sodden brute went so far, even before he violently struck her again and again, that, though he confirmed her in her abhorrence of the proposed union, he was the first great reforming force in her life. After *that*, she realised, she might "dry up." Foulness of speech could go no further. A disgust of it all came upon the girl. She prayed an unwonted prayer to that mysterious abstraction God, whose name she heard as often as that of the police, that she might have strength to refrain from all ugly horrors of speech, except, of course, such acknowledged ornaments of conversation as "bloody" and "damn."

Yet no, not quite the first, if the most immediate, reforming influence. She had already incurred the wrath and contempt of the Horsleydown and Irongate mudswipes, by her attitude towards Jim Shaw, a despised and hated "cat," a river policeman. He had saved her from drowning, on an occasion when the most obvious help lay with her own people, not one of whom, boy or man, had bestirred himself. "Water-rat" though she was, and acknowledged foe as was every "cat," she was so little at one with her kindred as to be able to feel grateful towards her saviour, particularly as he was so good-looking a deliverer, and possessed, in her eyes, a manner of ideal grace and dignity.

It was on a dirty, foggy, December afternoon that Dick Robins had tried, through a flood of blasphemy and obscenity, to drift his meaning alongside the wharf of the girl's mind. When he found that she would have none of it, was a rebel outright, he followed curses with blows, till at last, wild with rage and pain, Madge rushed from the low tavern whither her father had inveigled her. Naturally, she made straight for the river. Having sprung into a dingy, she sculled rapidly amidstream. She had no idea what she was going to do. To get quite away from that horrible street, from that drink-den, from that human beast who called himself her father — that was her one overmastering wish.

An unpleasant fate might easily have been hers that night, had she not fortunately broken an oar. The swing of the current caught the boat, and in a moment she was broadside on. A wood-barge and a collier were coming down, and a large steamer forging up-stream, and there she jobbled helplessly, right in their way, and almost certain to be crushed or swamped. All the girl's usual resourcefulness suddenly left her. She realised that she was done for, a thought at which not she but only her youth instinctively rebelled.

Suddenly, *slump — slump — splash* — came the wood-barge almost upon her. She saw a pole thrust past her to stave the dingy off from too violent a concussion; and the next moment some one was over the low side and in the boat beside her. She recognised Jim Shaw, as in a dream.

"Here, I'll put you right," he said roughly; "hand me that oar." While sculling from the stern-rollock, he told her that he had been up-stream on duty, and had been given a lift down again by his friend, the owner of the barge "Pride of Wapping;" that he had seen her predicament, and, as the distance narrowed, recognised her face; and that "there he was."

Madge thanked him earnestly, and remarked, incidentally, that "it *was* a bloody near squeak." She saw him look at her, and glanced back with a new, vague apprehension.

"You're a pretty girl, Madge, and a good girl, I believe, — too good to use that rot. Wy, blast me, if I 'eard a sister o' mine use that word 'bloody' so free permiskuous, I'd let her know — damme if I would n't!"

"*Have* you a sister, Mr. — Mr. — Shaw?" asked Madge, curiously, and not in the least offended.

"No, nor no mother, neither; but I had 'em. Look here, Madge, I'm a lonely chap, an' I've took a fancy to you — did that time I hauled ye out o' the Pool — and I'll tell you wot: you cut old Robins and all that gang, and be my gal?"

Madge turned her great eyes upon him. He thought she was scornful, or mayhap only reckoning up the actual and possible advantages of the connection. She, for her part, was taken aback by what seemed to her his splendid chivalry and the refined charm of his address.

"Now then, lass, say yes or no, for we'll be

along o' the Irongate in a jiffy, an' some o' your lot 's bound to be there."

"I 'll be your gal, Jim Shaw," was all she said, in a low voice.

Shaw thereupon gave the oar a twist, and kept the boat midstream for a hundred yards or so below Irongate wharf. When nearly opposite a small floating quay marked No. 9, he sculled alongside. Ten minutes later he had obtained leave of absence for the night, and then he and Madge went off together to hunt for lodgings.

For the next few days Madge was fairly happy. She would have been quite happy if she and Jim could have been with each other; but it was a busy time with the river-police, and he could not get away at nights. He got back to their room between six and eight in the morning, but had to sleep till well after midday; and as he had to be on duty again by six, and sometimes earlier, they had not much time for going anywhere together. But, in truth, Madge cared little for the entertainments they did go to. The painted tawdry women offended her in a way they had never done before; the coarse jokes of the men did not strike her as funny. She was dimly conscious of a great change in herself. Physically and mentally she was another woman after that first night alone with Jim. She was his "gal," and would be the mother of their "kid" if she had one; but it was not the obvious in wifehood or motherhood that took possession of her dormant imagination, but something mysterious, awful even, sacred. The outward sign of this spiritual revolution, this new, solemnising, exquisite obsession, was a complete cessation from even such customary flowers of speech as those above alluded to; and, later, a more scrupulous tidiness. What joy it was when Jim told her one morning that he was to have Boxing-day as a complete holiday. At last the heavens seemed opened. He proposed all manner of wild and extravagant trips: a visit to the inside of St. Paul's or the Tower, so familiar externally to both, to be followed by an omnibus-trip through the great city to that home of splendour, Madame Tussaud's, or even to the Zoological Gardens, the monkey-house in which had made on Jim's boyhood-mind an indelible impression of excruciating humour. The wildest suggestion of all was a triple glory: the Tower and St.

Paul's, then far away to the gorgeous delights of the Crystal Palace, and at night to the Pantomime at Drury Lane.

But in great happiness the mind sometimes resents superfluity of joys. In deep love, as in deep water, says a great writer, there is a gloom. The gloom, in the instance of Madge, arose from her profound weariness of the streets and the house-life, her overmastering longing for the river. If an angel had offered her a boon, she would have fulfilled a passionate dream by becoming a female member of the river-police, and being ranked as Jim Shaw's mate.

When Jim realised what was in the girl's mind and heart, he good-naturedly, though not without a sigh, gave up his projects, and bestirred himself to please Madge. One suggestion he did make: that they should get "spliced;" but Madge thought this a waste of time, money, and even welfare — for she vaguely realised that she had, and probably would continue to have, more hold over Jim as her "man" than as her legal husband. "It might be better," he remarked once, meditatively.

"But why; don't I love you?" was Madge's naïve and unanswerable reply.

By Christmas Day all was arranged. Jim knew the captain of a river steamer who had promised to take them as far as Kew. Thence they were to go by rail to Windsor, to show Madge those two marvels, — where the Queen lived, and "the real country;" then they were to leave in time to catch the ebb-tide below Richmond, and go down stream on a friend's hoy, the "Dancing Mary," all the way to Gravesend. Madge would thus see the country and the ocean in one day, and yet all the time be on the river. The project was a mental intoxication to her. She was in a dream by day, a fever by night. Jim laughingly told her that he would be blowed if he would ask for another holiday soon.

A memorable day, indeed, it proved. Madge's education received an almost perilously rapid stimulus. Long before dusk she had won for herself, besides a little rapture, a new pain that would henceforth be a constant ally, and perhaps a tyrant.

The beauty even of the winter-riverscape affected her painfully. That great stillness, that indescribable calm, that white peace, that stainless purity of the snowy vicinage of the

Thames near Windsor, was an overwhelming reproach upon life as she knew it, and upon herself. She was conscious of three emotions: horror of the past, gratitude to Jim, her saviour and revealer, and a dumb sense of the glory of life as it might be. But at first she was simply overcome. If she had not feared how Jim would take such folly, she would have screamed, if for nothing else than to break the silence. He had his pipe, merciful boon for the stagnant spirit and the inactive mind; she had nothing to distract her outer from her inner self, nothing to ease her from the dull perplexity and pain of that incessant if almost inarticulate soul-summons of which she was dimly conscious. More than once, even, a great home-sickness came upon her; a bodily nostalgia for that dirty, congested, often hideous, always squalid life, to which she had been born, and in which she had been bred. Once, at a lonely spot, where the river curved through snow-clad meadows, with an austere but exquisite beauty, she was conscious of a certain relief, when she and her fellow-passengers were collectively swept by a volcanic lava-flood of abuse from an infuriated bargee, horrible to most ears that heard, but to her coming as inland odours to tired seamen, subtly welcome as it was in its appealing home-sound.

She was affected as profoundly, if not so acutely, by the voyage down the lower reaches of the Thames beyond the Pool. Windsor itself had not greatly impressed her. It was too remotely grand.

When, late that night, the hoy anchored off Gravesend, and through the darkness came up a moan, and a sigh, and a tumult as of muffled steps and stifled whispers, that was the voice of the sea, Madge, almost for the first time in her life, was troubled by the thought of death. The night was dark, without moon, and the stars were obscured by drifted smoke and opaque films of mist. An easterly wind worried the waves as they came slap-slapping against the current, and there was often a sound as of irregular musketry. A steady *swish-swish* accompanied the now flowing tide, or the way of the wind. The salt chill that came with it made the girl's blood tingle. She longed to do something, she knew not what.

They had two berths to themselves, screened so efficiently as to give them all the privacy of a bedroom. They were very happy after their long wonderful day; but what with happiness, many pipefuls of tobacco, and liberal gin, Jim soon fell asleep. Madge lay awake for hours. It was a boisterous night seaward. The reach of the Thames estuary thereabouts was all in a jumble. The wind, surging overhead, had a cry in it foreign to any inland wail or city scream. Madge listened and trembled. The sound of the sea calling: it was a revelation, a memory, a prophecy, a menace.

II.

NEXT day, Madge learned what she had expected: that her voyage down-stream had been duly noted by her kindred. She knew them well enough to regret that she and Jim had not kept out of sight from, at any rate, London Bridge to the Isle of Dogs. Jim laughed at her fears, but warned her to hold her weather-eye open, and, in particular, to avoid the Pool.

This, unfortunately, was just what Madge could not do. She had the river-water in her blood. Jim might as well have put a mouse near a cheese and told it to stay beside the empty bread-plate.

Gradually she became a more and more frequent visitor to her old haunts. It was commonly understood, Irongate-way, that Madge had gone off with some seafaring chap, but was getting tired, or perhaps was not finding the "rhino" quite so free. On the other hand, her secret was known where she would fain have had it unguessed. She had a good deal to put up with. The female Poolites had nasty tongues; the males of the species, whom she had kept at bay before with comparative ease, believed that they might now have a turn. An unspoken but not less dreaded ban lay upon her on the part of her own people. Now and again she saw Ned Bull, and the savage lust in the man's brutal face, with a concurrent hatred and revengeful malice, sent all her nature into revolt. He caught her one day on Horsleydown stairs, and at once leered at her in devilish fashion and taunted her. She swung round and struck him full in the face.

The next moment she was in the water. When a sympathetic bystander had hauled her out — sympathetic in the sense that he wanted to see Bull "give the gal her change" in full — the man strode up and hissed in her ear, —

"I'll knife that bully-rip o' yourn as sure's I'm death on 'cats;' ay, an' wot's more, I'll 'ave you as my gal yet."

"Ay, Ned Bull," answered Madge, in a loud, clear voice, while her great eyes flashed dauntless defiance, "that you will when the Pool's run dry, an' I'm squeaking like a rat in the mud; but not afore that, s' 'elp me Gawd!"

After this episode Madge knew that she would have to be doubly on her guard. Ned Bull was not a man to have as an enemy, particularly as he knew well where to strike the only blow she really feared. And, as it happened, her fears ultimately proved to be only too well-grounded; though some months passed in apparent security.

The only one among all whom she knew, who had remained loyal to her, was a girl called Arabella Goodge, to whom she had once done a prompt service. The girl had sworn that she would never be content till she had proved her gratitude, and she meant it. The opportunity came at last.

Late one afternoon in June, just six months after her union with Jim, Madge was astonished to hear herself asked for at the door of her lodging. "Is this wheer Jim Shaw's gal lives?" was not tactful, perhaps, but it was unmistakable. Madge recognised the voice, and was eager to see one whom instinctively she knew to be a herald of good or evil; yet she could not but enjoy a delay which involved so personal a passage of arms as that which took place between Mrs. McCorkoran, the landlady, and

Miss Goodge. Ultimately Miss Goodge was announced into the presence of " Mrs. Shaw, an' Mrs. James Shaw at that, an' be damned t' ye!"

The girl came — and at what risk to herself no one could better know than Madge — to give warning of a plot. Two boats of " rats " were to lie in wait that very night, if the fog held, and run down the " Swiftsure," a particularly obnoxious " cat-boat." Of course Miss Goodge would not have troubled to track down and visit Madge merely to tell her an interesting item of news; only it happened that Jim Shaw was "stroke" in the " Swiftsure."

Madge realised the peril at once. She thanked Arabella cordially, and then set off for Jim's station. The news was doubly welcome to Jim; it meant promotion probably, as well as the excitement of a fight and of turning the tables.

The upshot was, that a boat with three or four dummy figures was at the right hour set adrift through the fog just above the appointed spot. The bait took. The collision took place, and Jim Shaw's dummy in particular suffered from concussion of the brain from an iron crowbar as well as from submersion in the river. The "rats" had scarcely realised how they had been befooled when the "Swiftsure" was upon them. There was a rush and struggle. The Pool-boat was upset, and each of the late occupants speedily nabbed, with the exception of Ned Bull,—an exception which Jim Shaw regretted personally for obvious reasons, and officially because that individual was particularly wanted at head-quarters, and his capture meant for the captor approval, and possibly promotion, by the powers that were.

Nevertheless, practical approval came. True, the crew of the "Swiftsure" were individually and collectively called "duffers" for having let Bull escape, when at least they might have hit him on the head with an oar: though to this Jim Shaw replied, and of course was backed up by his comrades, that Ned Bull must have sunk and been carried off in the undertow. A drowned Ned Bull was not so satisfactory as a caught Ned Bull; but still the fact was one for congratulation.

What most concerned Shaw was his promotion a grade higher. The superintendent who informed him of this rise further hinted that the young man was looked upon favourably, and that he might expect to get on, if he kept on acting on the square and was diligently alert for the wicked.

On his way home next morning, eager to tell Madge the good news, Jim pondered on how best to celebrate the occasion. Suddenly an idea occurred to him. Promotion and prospects have a stimulating effect on ethical conceptions. Jim decided, firstly, that he would make Madge his legal wife; secondly, that he would forgive his enemies and invite old Robins and Will of the "Jolly Rovers," and Bob Robins and his wife, and make a day or rather an evening of it. This, he was sure, would give Madge a position and importance which she could not otherwise have, while it was almost the only way (except the convenient if perilous one of double-dealing) to remove or at least to modify the resentment which Madge had incurred. Madge was delighted with his news. It meant another day, sometime, up the river; another night, Gravesend way, within sound of the sea; and, moreover, Jim could now carry out his fascinating projects in connection with Madame Tussaud's and the Crystal Palace. To the question of the marriage ceremony she preserved an indifferent front. If Jim really wished it, she of course was willing; if he did n't, it was equally the same to her. The girl, in fact, was one of those rare natures to whom the thing was everything and the symbol of no moment. But she was seriously opposed to Jim's Christian charity in the matter of the proposed wedding-party. She loved his sentimental weakness, but, with her greater knowledge of ineradicable depravity, she thought that the honour of her father's company might be dispensed with. She yielded at last to the suggestion as to her brother Bob and his wife, with a stipulation as to Arabella Goodge; but disparagingly combated the claims of her uncle. Being a woman, however, having begun yielding, she yielded all. Before Jim went off to the river that night, the marriage-day was fixed, and it was decided that, at the subsequent party at the aristocratic river-side tavern, the "Blue Boar," the company of Jim and his groomsman, Ted Brown, and of Madge and her bridesmaid Arabella Goodge, was to be further graced by Mr. Dick Robins (if sufficiently sober), Mr. and Mrs. Robert Robins, and Mr. William Robins of the "Jolly Rovers."

The marriage was to take place three weeks hence, as Jim was to get his long-promised holiday of a week, from the morning of Saturday the 18th of July till the evening of Friday the 24th. What a week this was to be! Three days of it were to be spent in the remote and wild country of Pinner, of which suburban locality Jim was a native, though he had not been there since he was a small boy. His aunt owned a small sweet-shop and general stationery business there, and would receive him and his bride for the slack days, Monday till Wednesday. As for the other days, the proposals of Madge were wild, those of Jim fantastically extravagant. The young man was more in love with Madge than ever, having the sense to see that she was one among a hundred or a thousand. Their life together had been a happy one for both. It was Jim, however, and not Madge who took a pleasurable interest in the fate of the child whose birth was expected in September.

It was on the 15th of July, just three days before the projected marriage, that Madge was startled, or at least perturbed, by an urgent message brought to her by a pot-boy from the

"Jolly Rovers." Her father was ill, dying, and wanted to see her at once.

Madge was neither hard-hearted nor a cynic, but it was with perfect sincerity that she remarked, *sotto voce*, "I'll be blowed if I'll rise to that fake." Later, however, something troubled her. A new tenderness, if also a new weariness, had come to her ever since she became daily and hourly conscious of the burden she bore within her. She was so much an unsullied child of nature, despite all her discoloured and distorted views of life, that this mystery of motherhood had all the astounding appeal of a new and extraordinary revelation. Jim's child and hers! The thought was strange and quiet as that winter-landscape she had seen once and never forgotten; though at times as strangely and overmasteringly oppressive as the silence of the starry sky, seen through the smoke or lifting fog, or above the flare of the gas-lamps in the street.

The upshot was that she set out for Plum Alley, off Thompson's Court, the trans-riverine home of her father, when he was not at the "Jolly Rovers" or elsewhere. On the way she called at the station to see Jim, but heard to her surprise that he was on special duty Horsley-down-way. She muttered that she might perhaps come across him, as she was just going there herself, — a remark which the superintendent heard disapprovingly. "Shaw's out on ticklish business, my girl," he said, kindly enough; "and it would be better if you were to keep out of his way: better for us, better for him, and better for you." All the same, Madge, as she went on her way, hoped she might at least get a glimpse of Jim. Since the "Swiftsure" incident she had never felt at ease when Shaw was on special duty. She was aware that Ned Bull, even if he was not drowned, had left a legacy of hate and revenge.

The July evening was heavy and sultry. The air was as though it consisted of a poisonous cloud of gin-flavoured human breath, with rank odours of divers kinds. In the narrow courts and alleys near the river the heat was stifling. The thunder, which all afternoon had growled menacingly round the metropolitan skirts beyond Muswell Hill and Highgate, had stolen past the eastern heights of Hampstead and crawled through the murky gloom of the town till it rested, sulkily brooding, from Pimlico to Blackfriars.

As Madge crossed the river, and stood for a few minutes to look longingly at the water, she noticed first that the tide was just on the turn of the ebb, and next that a thick, sultry fog, scarce less dense than a typical "London mixture," was crawling stealthily up-stream from Shoreditch and Wapping. She was thinking of Jim, and was rather glad that he was on shore-duty.

When at last she reached Plum Alley, she found, somewhat to her surprise, that her father really awaited her. On the other hand, she saw at a glance that his "sudden illness" was a "fake."

Dick Robins, however, did not give his daughter time for an indignant retreat, much less for reproaches.

"Look 'ere, girl," he began hoarsely, "your brother Bob's in trouble, an' you're the only blarsted swipe as can 'elp 'im. S' 'elp me Gawd, this yere is true, ev'ry word on it, an' no fake. Wot? eh? W'ere is 'ee? Wy, 'ee's down China Run way. 'Ee's waitin' there. Waitin' for wot? Wy, blarst — I mean 'ee's awaitin' fur the stranger. Wot stranger? Wy, the stranger as you've to run down through the fog to the Isle o' Dogs."

Hoarse explanations, with remonstrances on the part of Madge, ensued, but at last she both understood and agreed. She had been brought up in full recognition of that cardinal rule that many things have to be done in life without knowing the why and the wherefore. She believed in the present emergency, and understood why the task of conveying the stranger downstream could be intrusted to no Poolite under a cloud. She was to go down to the sadly miscalled Larkwhistle Wharf, where she would find a boat in charge of a man. In the stern would be the "bundle." She was not to speak to this "bundle" on any account, and was not to worry "it" with curious looks. She was to row down-stream till off Pig Point in the Isle of Dogs, and wait off shore till another boat joined her, and relieved her of her freight. The man, a friendly lighterman, would act as look-out and bow-pilot.

"Wot about the weddin', father?" said Madge, somewhat reluctantly, as she was about to leave.

Mr. Robins put down the bottle of "Aunt Maria," from which he had just taken a hoarse gurgling, salival swig.

"Oh — ah — to be sure — wot about the weddin'! Ha, ha! Well, I'm blarsted if I know if my noomerous parlyhairymentary dooties — *hiccough and choke* — Yes, by Goramity, I'm bl...."

Madge did not wait to hear any more. She had done her duty so far, and the sooner the rest of it was fulfilled the better content would she be.

She could not leave, however, without a parting shot. Dick Robins heard her voice as she vanished down-stairs: "Remember, father, if you and 'Aunt Maria' come together on Saturday, you won't be allowed in!"

When she reached Larkwhistle Wharf she was perspiring heavily. The brooding thunder overhead, the stagnant atmosphere, the airless, suffocating fog, made existence a burden and action a misery. Movement on the water, however, promised some relief.

There was no one on the wharf, nothing beside it except a boat in which a muffled figure crouched in the stern-sheets, with a tall man seated upright in the bow. This was her boat, clearly.

As she stepped across the gunwale, Madge

started and trembled. For a moment she thought she recognised, in the silent surly lighterman, no other than Ned Bull; but when she saw that he looked away, indifferent so far as she was concerned, and noticed that his hair was black and curly, and that he had a long beard, her sudden suspicion and fear lapsed into mere uneasiness. As for the other passenger, he was evidently determined to betray himself neither by word nor by gesture.

In silence, save for the occasional splash of an oar and the steady gurgling wash at the bows, Madge rowed the boat down-stream. Thrice she was unpleasantly conscious of the hot breath of the lighterman upon her cheek; at the third time, and without looking round, she quietly asked him to keep a steady look-out in front of him, as in such a fog an accident might occur at any moment.

At last she guessed that she was off the Isle of Dogs. She was glad. Not only was she exhausted with the heat and labour, but somewhat anxious now about the condition of the boat, a rotten tub at the best. It had begun to leak, and the chill muddy water clammed her ankles. Suddenly, through the fog, she heard the lighterman give a peculiar double-whistle. Almost immediately afterwards a boat, rowed swiftly by two men, shot alongside.

The next moment the lighterman was aboard the new-comer. Once seated, he leaned over and whispering hoarsely to Madge to row straight on, after turning the boat's bow shoreward, told her that as soon as she came to a pier she was to let the other passenger out. The man had scarce finished speaking before he and his companions became invisible in the mist.

Madge was again alarmed. The voice, surely, was the voice of Ned Bull. She could have sworn to it, and yet — ?

Wiping the sweat from her forehead, and pausing on her oars for a moment to listen to the distant moan and billowy hollow roar of the thunder, which had at last broken its brooding silence, she noticed suddenly that the leakage was rapidly becoming serious. The water was high above her ankles, and was swiftly rising. A gurgling sound behind her betrayed where the danger lay. The boat had been plugged, and the plug had just recently been removed!

Barely had she realised this when the dingy raked up against a jagged spike, and began to settle down.

She knew it all now, all except the mystery of this taciturn, moveless stranger. So, Ned Bull was to have his revenge. But the need of prompt action brought all her energies into play. "Now then, you there," she cried angrily to her mute fellow-passenger, "you've got ter move if you don't want to fill yer boots wi' bottom-mud. We're sinkin', d'ye 'ear? . . . . Drat the bloomin' cove, 'ee's asleep! Hi!"

But here there was a lurch and a rush of water. The boat collapsed, as though it were a squeezed sponge.

No sooner had Madge found her breath after her submersion than she struck out towards and made a dive for her companion, who was evidently unable to swim, and was fast drowning.

A minute later she had grasped him by his rags. She was conscious at the same moment of a red light piercing the gloom: the bow-light of a barge-bug churning splutteringly against the current and towing a half-empty hoy up-stream. She gave a loud cry for help, and then another that was more like a shriek. The second was the result of a discovery that she had just made. The body in her grip was not that of a living man, nor even of a man who had just died. It was a corpse, stiff and chill.

The shock terrified her. For a moment she believed that she had been made accessory to some foul murder. She let go of the hideous bundle of rag-clothed flesh she was upholding as best she could. Another moment, and the corpse would have been sucked under and swept down-stream: a vague instinct made Madge suddenly reach forward and grip the body again.

The lights of the tug and the green and red lanterns of the hoy now streamed right upon her. Weighted as she was with her soaked clothes, and the burden of her close on seven months' motherhood, she struggled not only to withstay the current, which fortunately was sweeping her steadily towards the hoy, but to keep the corpse from sinking until at least she could see it clear. Still, the strain was too great, and she was just about to let go, when a broad ray of light flashed full athwart the dead face.

It was that of Jim Shaw, her husband.

For a moment the world reeled. Death called to her out of the windy darkness overhead, out of the rushing river, out of the sea-reaches beyond; Death sang in her ears, and held her body and soul as in a vice; Death was in her heart, in her brain, on her lips, in the dull glaze of her staring eyes.

Suddenly a mad rage swept her back into the tide of agony that was life. With a swift gesture she raised the head of the corpse, and stared wildly into the lightless unrecognising eyes. The wash of the water and her grasp had loosened the rags in which Jim had been disguised, and she saw the purple bruise and gaping knife-thrust wound through which his young life had gone.

With a long terrible cry of despair Madge let go the body of her beloved, and herself sank back into the water, as a dying woman, after a last flicker of life, might fall back into the pillows. If all had occurred a little earlier or a little later, she would have been drowned then and there, and have suffered no more.

The man at the helm on the tug-boat caught sight of her, and yelled to the man at the bow of the hoy. The bargeman missed her, owing to the rapid slush and surge of the churned water alongside; but his comrade at the stern caught at the swirling clothes with a bill-hook, and in a few minutes she was lying unconscious on the deck of "The Golden Hope." Her rescuers had seen nothing of the rowboat, nor even of the body to which she had clung; but they strained their eyes and ears lest any other unfortunates should be in need of succour.

It was fortunate for Madge that there was a woman on board. The wife of the master of "The Golden Hope" was not, like so many of the Poolites, merely a female, but a true woman.

In the middle of the night, just before the break of dawn, a man-child was prematurely born into the world, in the stuffy deck-house of the barge. It was born dead: "an' a precious good thing too, drat it for its imperence in a-coming where it wasn't wanted," as Mrs. Hawkins of "The Golden Hope" philosophically remarked. She had understood at once that the new-comer was not born in lawful wedlock. Had the little one lived, had it even been born alive and breathed feebly for a brief season, the good woman would not only have lamented its decease, but would have kept close to the letter of the law. As it was, she had a hurried colloquy with her husband, a circumlocutory argument to the effect that the poor young mother might as well be saved all the shame and trouble, and perhaps worse.

Mr. Peter Hawkins listened gravely, nodded once or twice in an uninterested way, spat once cautiously, then again meditatively, and, finally, emphatically. He left the deck-house, and in a minute or two returned with a large and heavy brick.

The dawn broke as "The Golden Hope" entered and passed through the Pool. A soft tender wave of daffodil light blotted out the eastern stars. The rigging and masts of the vessels at the docks and in the river became magically distinct, and the red and yellow lanterns flared gaudily. Here and there a green lantern-light danced along a narrow surface of dark water fast turning into a hue of slate. A dull noise came from the city on either side, though it seemed asleep.

On the river there was silence, save for an indiscriminate grinding noise from a large

Baltic screw steamer, timed to sail at sunrise; and, on a China tea-clipper, a Malay singing shrilly, with fantastic choric variations of a strange uncanny savagery.

As the barge slump-slushed through the deepest part of the Pool, a small packet was dropped overboard. It sank immediately. This package was, in the view of Mr. and Mrs. Hawkins, a cold little body with a heavy brick tied round its feet; to its mother, who had just returned to full consciousness, the burial was as that of her own joy, her own life.

Madge was much too weak to move, even if kindly Mrs. Hawkins had hinted that her absence would be preferable to her company. The woman had taken a fancy to the poor lass, with her great eyes filled with grief and longing and despair, with at times, too, a wild light which looked like passionate hate.

She had had a talk with her husband, and had decided to keep Madge with them till the barge reached Sunbury, where she had a sister, who in the summer months kept a small tea and ale house for her own benefit and the refreshment of cheap trippers and wayfarers. There she would leave the girl for a time, in care of Polly 'Awkins. If Madge could pay for her keep so much the better; if not, why then o' God's grace she and Polly betwixt them would provide for her for a bit till she could look round.

And at Sunbury in due course poor Madge was left. She had become a different woman in the few days which succeeded the death of Jim and the premature birth and loss of the child of their love. A frost had come over her youth. She was so still and strange that, at first, good, kindly, superabundantly stout Miss Hawkins was quite awed by her. The woman's generous kindness at last broke down the girl's reserve, and the whole story was confided to her. There was something so romantic in it to Polly Hawkins, the very breath of wild romance indeed, that, for all her disapproval and misapprehension of Madge's action in the matter of a legalised union, she was completely won over. Never, even in the "Family Astounder" or the "West End Mirror," monthly parts or old bound volumes of which she was wont to pore over in the winter nights, had she come across anything that stirred her so much. But she passed from her high vicarious excitement into something resembling the emotional state of a participant in a tragedy in real life, when, one wild rain-swept evening late in August, all the bitter pain and agony and passion of Madge's ruined life broke out in revolt.

She had only one wish now, she declared, only one object: to be revenged on her father, and, above all, on Ned Bull. She was no longer a girl with a haven of happiness ahead; she was a wrecked woman, with a choice between going to pieces on the breakers or being engulfed in a quicksand. Since all was ruin ahead, was she to surrender everything, to go tamely hence, a victim with no will or power of retribution? No, she swore, as with flashing eyes and erect figure she moved to and fro in the kitchen parlour, she would not be content till she had made her father pay *her* for his crime, pay with his life, and till she saw Ned Bull swing on the gallows.

Miss Hawkins saw that she was in earnest; passionately, insanely in earnest; and she trembled. She had come to love the girl, and though her departure would be a loss both to her and her pocket (for Madge had communicated with Jim's comrades, who had raised a handsome subscription for her when they found that officially nothing could be done), she would not be ill at ease. But now — now it would be to let a murderess loose. Why, some day it would all be in the papers! A prospective perusal of certain head-lines brought out a cold perspiration upon her neck and forehead: " 'Orrible murder in the Docks," "Last Confession," "Execution of Madge Robins," "What did the Bargee do with the Baby?" "Testimony of Polly Hawkins," and so forth.

Miss Hawkins rose, looked at Madge in fear and trembling and deep admiration, all merged in a profound and loving pity. But she had not the gift of expression, and all she could say was: "My dear, 'ave some black-currant cordial."

Madge, however, understood. The tears broke out in a flood from her eyes, and with sobs and a shaking frame she threw herself in the arms of her friend.

The following day was a Sunday. As much for distraction as for any other reason, Miss Hawkins persuaded Madge to go with her to church. Madge had never been in a church, and for the first part of the service she was too shy and bewildered to understand, much less to enjoy, what she saw and heard. The singing soothed her, and some of the prayers left haunting echoes in her brain. The clergyman was that rare individual, a fervent Christian and a perfectly simple man, who did not fulfil his priestly duties perfunctorily, but as though he were a wise and loving gardener watering the precious flowers of a strict but beloved Master. She followed, or cared to follow, very little of what he said; but his earnestness impressed her. Through all his discourse sounded, like the wild moan and wail of the sea-wind, the words of his text: "Forgive us our sins, as we forgive our enemies." "Then shall we be together with the Lord" were the last words she heard the vicar utter, before the congregation rose at the benediction.

In discussing the matter later with Miss Hawkins she did not gain much enlightenment. Miss Hawkins said that religion was meant to be took like gin, with a good allowance of water. "It did n't do to take things jist as they were spoke.

"Vicars an' sich like were paid same as other

folk, an' their business was to deal out salvation dashed wi' hell-fire.

"My dear," she added, "there's nary a man livin', be he a vicar or only a Ranting Johnny, who does n't promise us more of both one and the other than there's any need for."

Madge did not sleep much that night. She was vaguely troubled. The fire of her wrath burned low, and though she heaped coals of remembrance upon it the flare-up was a failure.

At breakfast next morning she asked Miss Hawkins abruptly if she had heard the vicar say "Forgive us our sins, as we forgive our enemies," and, if so, what she thought of it.

Miss Hawkins finished her tea. Meditatively she scooped out the sugar and slowly refilled the cup.

"Not much," she said.

The rest of the meal was taken in silence. The day was so glorious that Madge wandered forth into a field near the river, unwittingly elate with returning youth and strength, and quick to answer to the sun's summons to the blood and the spirit.

She lay for a long time through the noon

heat, instinctively revelling in the flood of sunshine. The sky was a dome of deepening blue, flecked with a few scattered greymare's-tails; the meadows were lush with the second hay and autumnal wild-flowers. Beyond her feet the river swept slowly by, the golden light falling along its surface and at once transmuted into silver and azure; while at the margins the overhanging trees threw a cloud of flickering green shadows into the moving movelessness below.

It was almost happiness to lie there so quietly, and watch the swallows swooping to and fro, the cows standing knee-deep in the shallows and flapping lazily their long tails, the purple dragon-fly shooting from reedy pool to pool. For the time being, the agony of remembrance was dulled.

More and more Madge perplexed herself by pondering over what she had heard in church. She had never felt as she had done to-day. There was a new peace, a new hope almost, in her troubled mind, though it had not yet taken definite form. The strange and baffling concourse of her thoughts, however, left her weary. The whole ebb and flow found expression, perhaps, in the sole words she spoke aloud, —

"No, that I can't: I can't make much of it. But I do see that going back to that hell of life at the Pool, even wi' letting my father be, an' knockin' out the knifin' o' Ned Bull an' leavin' 'im, as the parson says, to Goramity, is not the way to get alongside o' Jim again, let alone that babby wich he'll 'ave 'igh an' dry sure as dixey."

It was nigh upon sundown before Madge clearly saw her way of salvation. "She'd got to die somehow;" but all her instincts were in revolt against that inevitable transference to the earth which would be her fate if death came upon her at Polly Hawkins's or any other house. "She couldn't abide the land: she knew *that:* not for all the blessedness of it ten times over."

Shortly before sunset she descried a boy going along the Sunbury towpath. She called him, and for sixpence he readily agreed to write a pencilled note at her dictation and thereafter deliver it to Miss Hawkins.

When the boy was gone, Madge waited a little while. She watched the sun grow large and red, and fall through the river-haze into the very middle of the river-reaches higher up. Then she found herself listening intently to a corncrake calling hoarsely close by through the tall wheat.

It seemed so little to do, and after all so little even to say farewell to.

A brief while after sunset a great red and yellow hoy, with a tattered brown sail outspread aloft to catch what breeze there was that would help the slow current, came heavily down-stream. It was laden with rye, and the man and boy on deck were drowsy with the heat and labour of the day. Neither of them felt the slight shock when the dilapidated bow-keel caught upon some obstruction.

It was late that night when the "Lively Nancy," in tow of a fat, unwieldy little barge-bug, slumped heavily through the jumble in the Pool. There was a heavy slashing criss-cross of water above, and, below the surface, a serpentine twisting and dovetailing, with cruel downward suctions. The tide was running up like a mill-race; the river-current and a high westerly wind tore their way seaward.

In this fierce conflict the bent keel of the

"Lively Nancy" was at last cleared of its obstruction.

For an hour or more thereafter, till the river-police discovered it, a woman's body was tossed to and fro in the Pool, idly drifting and bumping against the slimy piers, along the gaunt, deserted wharves.

THE COWARD.

The Coward:

An Episode of the Franco-Arab War.

THERE was not an eddy of air, yet through the darkness of a clouded night the sound of water in motion was audible. As Colonel Le Marchant, mounted on his white Arab, a present from the Sheik of Touaroua, listened intently, he could hear that the slight wish-wash of the water did not come from the margin of the Chott. Clearly, the sound was from far out on the stillness of the vast placid lake. An immense breath came from the desert. There was no wind, and the silence was terrible: yet in that muffled breath, that sigh, there were many suspirations. To the south of the Chott, sand, — leagues of stony, herbless sand; to the east, sand, long rolling hills of desert-surf become hard as marl; to the west, sandy pastures, freshening ever and again to green spaces, with small oases many leagues distant from each other, the desert itself stretching at last across the frontier of Morocco to where Figuig lay, the "boon of the wanderer;" to the north, scanty pasture-lands, commanded by the military station of El Khadthera, the oasis of Sidi Khalifa, sacred to fanatics, and the hill-villages below Saida, future capital of the South-Oranian Atlas.

From the south, from the east, from the west, from the north, came that vague breath through the silence. The panther and the jackal moved along the northerly margins of the Chott, for the wind had been from the south, and that way still sniffed the antelopes, clustered in tremulous groups beyond the tall sedges where they could hear the wild boar snorting and stamping. Night-wayfarers, mounted on *mecharis* or leading their camels in long lines, passed unseen along the sandy ways, eager to gain haven, if possible, ere the storm should break.

The storm which was feared, however, was not of the atmosphere. Rumor had gone abroad that Bou-Amama Bel-Arbi had not only openly defied the hated French usurpers, but had drawn into ambush an officer of the all-powerful *Bureau Arabe* with his escort, and slain every infidel of the company. This meant war; and, in war, peaceful travellers were subject to spoliation from friends and foes alike. Provisions, transport; neither the French coming from El Riod, from Saida, or from El Khadthera, nor the insurgent Arabs under the Man of God, Bou-Amama, could be expected to resist temptation in the hour of need.

But by the island in the narrow strait, to the north of the great Chott El Chergui, no one passed. Colonel Le Marchant, it is true, underwent threefold risk by adventuring there at that hour and alone; but in the very circumstances that conduced to these risks lay also sufficient warrant of safety.

Eugène François Le Marchant was a man of proved courage, familiar with the vicissitudes of military life in Algeria, with the perils of man-hunting and wild-sport in the Sahara. If he feared anything this night, it was not the lion or the panther that might venture on a sudden rearward attack; still less the stealthy

Arab marauder, or roaming Touareg; not even insurgent tribesmen already leagued with or on their way to join this fanatic Bou-Amama Bel-Arbi, with his Allah-inspired mission to drive the French from the southlands. His fear was that he might be seen of some of his comrades or troops from El Khadthera.

Had the night been clear, he would not have ridden to his rendezvous on his conspicuous white charger, but have come later, in disguise, and covertly. As it was, he knew that in the obscurity of this thunder-heavy night *Vent-du-Paradis* would not be recognisable fifty yards away, while in the unequalled swiftness of the beautiful mare was prompt escape from any sudden emergency.

As he leaned from his saddle, and listened with suspended breath, he gave at last a sigh of relief.

A few minutes later, the wash on the Chott having passed into a steady swish-swish, a clumsy boat, little better than a side-boarded raft, grounded in the sand, within a few feet from where the white mare impatiently sniffed the air and pawed the loose soil.

"Is that you, Abdallah?" he asked in a low voice, and in Arabic.

"It is I, *Moulai*."

"Where is Nakhala?"

"She is not with me. Nay, *Sidi*, do not curse: I tell you the truth. The Blind Sheik went north this morning."

"What, has Mahomet El-Djebeli gone to join Bou-Amama?"

"Even so."

"May Allah keep him blind through all eternity! What has he done with Nakhala?"

"She too has gone — of course."

"What message do you bring?"

"Mahomet El-Djebeli is of the tribe of the Ouled-Sidi-Sheikh."

"What does that mean?"

"That he will do the bidding of him who is now chief of his tribe as well as leader of the Faithful. What Bou-Amama Bel-Arbi says, that will Mahomet-ibn-Mahomet-Eb-Djebel fulfil. And Bou-Amama has bidden Mahomet give his adopted daughter Nakhala to Si Suleiman ben Khaddour."

A deep curse broke from the lips of Colonel Le Marchant. For a few moments thereafter there was silence, save for the slight ripple of the water of the Chott, the restless pawing of

Vent-du-Paradis, and the distant howling of a jackal.

"Suleiman ben Khaddour is our sworn ally," he said at last, in a harsh voice. "Is it not true that even now he is at Ain Sifi-sifa, keeping an eye on those rebellious fellows at Géryville?"

Abdallah shifted uneasily, and muttered some evasive reply.

"Well," resumed the Colonel, "I will soon find something for Suleiman to do. Tell me now what else Nakhala said."

"That she will try and see you, about an hour before dawn, at the place of the fallen columns, to the north of the village of Sidi Khalifa."

Colonel Le Marchant could not repress a sound of triumph.

"She will come alone — she will be alone, of course?"

"I have given you her words, *Moulai.*"

"Good. Go now, Abdallah. Come to me to-morrow afternoon, and I will give you what will more than recompense you for all you have done for me. But when you leave here I wish you to go straight to Ain Sifi-sifa.

Seek Si Suleiman ben Khaddour, and tell him that I wish his advice, and that he is to repair to El Khadthera early to-morrow."

"But, Sidi Col'nell, Si Suleiman is —"

"What?"

Again Abdallah muttered indistinctly, and made a noise with his oar as though to distract attention.

"What did you say, Abdallah?"

"I said, you have but to command, *Moulai*."

"Now, go; and be wary. One moment, Abdallah. Suppose Nakhala cannot come, or if anything should prevent my getting to the Ruins in time for the appointment, where shall I seek her?"

But by this time Abdallah had oared his craft a few yards away.

"Under the green flag of Bou-Amama Bel-Arbi," he cried, as guardedly as possible: adding, below his breath, " or, dog of a Roumi, in the arms of Si Suleiman."

A few seconds more, and the Arab was out of sight in the darkness that brooded over the Chott and the surrounding waste. Colonel Le Marchant walked his mare a few steps, and then drew rein again, pondering deeply.

Suddenly *Vent-du-Paradis* threw back her head, and sniffed anxiously, while with swift uneasy motion she pawed the sand and switched her long white tail to and fro.

The Colonel leant forward, and listened intently. There was not a sound suggestive of any one or anything approaching, not a yellow spark of flame anywhere from crouching panther or hyena. Nevertheless, the mare became more and more uneasy.

With a sudden cry the horseman brought his spurs against her flanks, and at the same time shook free the bridle.

Vent-du-Paradis swung as if on a pivot, and the next moment shot through the gloom like a flash of white summer-lightning.

In less than a minute a strange thing happened. Two of the innumerable small sand-hillocks near the margin of the Chott collapsed, and simultaneously a black mass emerged from each.

Two Arabs, young men, almost nude, cautiously approached each other, one evidently in some pain, though not seriously hurt — he whom the French colonel's mare had trampled upon in the first spring of her flight.

A few words were rapidly interchanged; then both disappeared in the gloom, one running swiftly to the west of El Khadthera and the other taking the more circuitous eastern route.

Meanwhile Colonel Le Marchant rapidly approached the fort. As he rode, he made up his mind what he would do. War, he argued, was inevitable now that poor Lieutenant Wimbrenner and his company had been snared and massacred by Bou-Amama. So, despite the urgent instructions sent to him from his superior officer at Tiaret, to keep the peace at all hazards till the French forces could be strengthened, and above all to conciliate the tribesmen of Géryville and the neighbourhood (among whom Si Suleiman ben Khaddour was the most influential man in authority), he persuaded himself that what would practically be his abduction of Mahomet El-Djebeli's adopted daughter would not be an act of treasonable selfishness. In fact, he added, with a grim smile, Nakhala would be a splendid hostage, for with this beautiful desert-princess in his possession he could control the wily and dreaded Suleiman ben Khaddour.

His heart beat quicker as he thought of

Nakhala, and of every incident connected with her since first they had met and he had heard her story.

Some three months back he had ridden out alone to the village-oasis of Sidi Khalifa. He had spent an evening hour with the Sheik Okba, and, on leaving, had found himself in the company of Mahomet El-Djebeli, who, with his family, was returning to the village of Ain Sifi-sifa. The Blind Sheik, as Mahomet was generally called, was a Moor of ancient Tlemçen lineage. In his younger days he had been resident as a trader among the Spaniards of Oran, and had even made a journey to the southern Spanish ports and cities. In common with many of the better-class Oranian Moors, he spoke Spanish fluently and could converse in French.

During the time of God's curse upon the land — the awful years of pestilence and famine, 1866 and 1867, when over two hundred thousand victims perished untimely — Mahomet El-Djebeli was in the region known as the Metidja. His life was saved by a Spanish settler, who not only nursed him through an attack of the dreaded cholera, but gave him shelter and employment. Early in 1867 occurred the earthquake which destroyed the most prosperous villages of the neighbourhood. The farm of Perey Valera was laid in ruins, and the worthy Spaniard killed in his attempt to save his dying wife from among the débris of his tottering walls. The sole thing that Mahomet found amid the desolation that had been Perey Valera's prosperity was his patron's only child, the little five-year old Dolores. No one claimed the child; no one would have anything to do with her, for Valera's ruin was complete, alas, even before the earthquake had wrought its culminating havoc.

Thus it was that Mahomet El-Djebeli took Dolores Valera as his adopted daughter. He went first to his own people on the lower slope of the Djebel Toumzait near Tlemçen, and there married.

Thereafter he went to Cherchel on the sea-coast, but was driven thence by the French, with whom he had come in conflict. He settled at a village near Milianah. There occurred the tragedy which altered his life. A French colonist somehow saw and fell in love with his wife, and when Mahomet found that Marghya had been unfaithful with the *colon*, he waited his opportunity for revenge, and ultimately killed them both. He fled for his life, but he took the little Dolores with him. It was shortly after this that the last outbreak of the insurrection of 1871 took place. The chief insurgents were the hill-tribesmen of the Beni-Manassir, and the foremost rebel was Mahomet-ed-Toumzait. After the revolt was finally crushed, there was no peace for the outlaw in the upper provinces. He made his way to the Oranian Sahara, and became an adopted member of the Ouled-Sidi-Sheikh. A year or two before he lost his sight through a gun-accident, he had taken two wives unto himself, though neither for his wives nor any one did he care aught in comparison with Dolores. No longer, however, could he endure the infidel name. As the girl was so beautiful and of extraordinary grace, she seemed to him like a young date-palm, "a thing of joy and rich promise of peace," in the words of Abd-El-Kadr, the poet-patriot; and so he called her Nakhala.

With years, Mahomet of Toumzait had learned wisdom. Though he hated the French, he saw that their power was great and that Allah permitted them to rule in the land. As Mahomet El Djebeli, one of the leaders of the Ouled-Sidi-Sheikh, he was safe from the vengeance of French law. And at the time when he visited the Sheik Okba of Sidi Khalifa, and met the *Roumi-Cheik* Le Marchant, there were reasons why he wished to cultivate pleasant relations with the foreign commander.

Thus, instead of resenting the presence of Colonel Le Marchant on the night-journey from Sidi Khalifa, Mahomet was courteously urgent in his invitation. The French officer was eager, on his part, to win the good will of a man who could be either a useful ally or a troublesome enemy.

But when half way to Ain Sifi-sifa an unlooked-for episode happened. A band of marauding Touaregs had made their way northward, and, in the cloudy night, had surrounded the small party of wayfarers. Colonel Le Marchant, hearing the screams of a woman close by him, was amazed to hear it followed by an appeal to him first in Spanish, then in French. The next moment he saw a girl of extraordinary beauty by his side, and, scarce thinking what he was doing, lifted her on to his high Moorish saddle. The rest of the party was almost overpowered. Drawing his revolver, Le Marchant soon disposed of the two Touaregs nearest him, and the next moment was out and away upon the desert.

He reached El Khadthera with his beautiful burden, though not to see much more of her; for, on the morrow, Mahomet El-Djebeli appeared, having bought his freedom from his captors. Nevertheless, there had been time for her rescuer to learn Nakhala's story, and to fall hopelessly, passionately, in love with the Spanish daughter of the Blind Sheik. The love was returned, and from the first moment. Eugène Le Marchant was her hero and lover from the moment when, with his strong arm round her, he had galloped away from the Touaregs. True, Mahomet speedily veiled her and took her back to his home, but already Nakhala had become Dolores. Love called to love, and, also, blood to blood. The twain had pledged each other, with solemn words of fealty.

Thereafter, Le Marchant had seen the girl three or four times, but with difficulty and serious peril. Their passion grew apace. It had become a flame to withstand the wind of death itself when the fanatic Bou-Amama suddenly preached his *Djehad*, and, a few weeks later, massacred Lieutenant Wimbrenner of the *Bureau Arabe* and his small escort. The anti-French feeling was at its height, even among the still nominally loyal tribesmen. Mahomet El-Djebeli forbade any communication between his people and the *Roumi*.

Through a step-brother of Nakhala's, Abdallah, sworn to secrecy and won to service, Colonel Le Marchant sent word to his beautiful Dolores that at last he would hesitate no longer, but take her as his bride in the face of any opposition or peril. She was to send word through Abdallah as to how and when and where they were to meet to this end.

It was for this message that, on this sultry evening in April, Colonel Le Marchant had ridden out of El Khadthera — or El Kreider, as the French call it — and, notwithstanding the earnest remonstrance of Major Cazin, without escort.

It did not take long for *Vent-du-Paradis* to reach the fortified village. As the Colonel passed the three sentries of the outer lines he asked of each if he had seen any one come or go since he, the Colonel, had ridden out. It was with satisfaction he learned that no one had been seen.

When he reached his quarters he astonished his orderly by the request to have *Vent-du-Paradis* ready at his door two hours before dawn. Within, he found Major Cazin, poring anxiously over a despatch just to hand, calling for immediate care on the part of the garrison of El Khadthera. Bou-Amama had not been content with his victory over poor Wimbrenner, but had sacked the French settlements, and was carrying ruin over a wide region: and it was now doubtful if he would wait Colonel Le Mason's column marching from Tiaret. In this event, he might be expected to retreat towards the Sahara with his booty and captives, either to rouse the tribes in a more thorough manner, or to foil his pursuers till the summer fully set in. It was advisable to prevent this, even apart from the imperative need to rescue the captives, the greater portion of whom were French and Spanish women.

No one knows what passed between Colonel

Le Marchant and Major Cazin; but, certainly, high words arose when the latter strongly pressed the immediate despatch of troops to occupy the village of Sidi Khalifa, particularly now that, as the Major had just learned, the Sheik Okba had been joined by Mahomet El-Djebeli.

"At the first sight of our troops," he urged, "Mahomet and his followers will decamp. Not a man, woman, or child will be left in Sidi Khalifa. It would be a good riddance, for the place is a hotbed of treason and fanaticism, and, once destroyed, things would go better here, even apart from that bloodthirsty devil, Bou-Amama."

This, however, was just what Colonel Le Marchant wished to avoid at all hazard. If Nakhala were to slip from his grasp now he might never see her again.

As a counter-movement he proposed sending out at once a detachment to Ain Sifi-sifa to "bring in" Si Suleiman ben Khaddour.

"Good heavens, *mon colonel*," exclaimed Major Cazin, exasperated, "that would be the signal for revolt all over the North-Sahara. In a few days there would not be a Frenchman left alive on this side of the Atlas or the Aurès. As it is, our countrymen at Géryville are in hourly peril of their lives."

"Nonsense, Major. Come ... excuse my brusqueness, but I know what I am about. I am determined to have this fellow Suleiman under my eye. I have already, as a matter of fact, ordered him to come here to-morrow."

Thus much was overheard. It was after this that angry words arose between the two officers, with the result that Major Cazin left his colonel in high dudgeon and went straight to his own apartment, refusing word with any one.

Eugene Le Marchant did not even attempt to sleep that night. To and fro he walked with feverish restlessness. Perhaps the thought of the wrong he was about to do Dolores Valera troubled him more than the probable and more immediate consequences of his projected act; for though the lady in Paris with whom he had made an unhappy marriage had practically separated from him, she was none the less still his wife. Yet perhaps no such regret perturbed him. He said over and over again, arguing with himself, that the girl loved him; that she was not an Arab but a European, and was necessarily wretched in her present circumstances; that now more than ever she would be miserable if he deserted her; that as his mistress she would be far happier than she could be as the wife of Si Suleiman; that even in the event of *that* failing she would still be better rather than worse off. All that he said was more than merely probable; but none the less he realised that he was not going to give Dolores any option.

Again and again he looked at his watch to see if the moment of his departure were at hand. At last the time came. He looked carefully at his revolver once more, descended, gave some directions to his orderly, and then sprang into the saddle.

The sentries who saw and recognised *Vent-du-Paradis* were astonished. The orders against any man, even an officer, leaving the fort after midnight and before sunrise, were imperative. But, granting the necessity for what almost seemed a forlorn-hope rider, why should the emissary be the Colonel himself?

Unheeding their probable questionings among themselves, Colonel Le Marchant rode steadily forward. He knew that the journey would occupy nearly an hour, for though Sidi Khalifa was at no great distance, the old Roman ruins where he was to meet Nakhala were to the north-west of the oasis, and had to be reached by a circuitous detour. He had to ride carefully, for not only did the route lie across a rough, uneven, and occasionally dangerously ravined country, but there was momentary peril of a surprise on the part of stray followers or would-be adherents of Bou-Amama.

When, at last, he drew rein close to a confused heap of fallen columns and blocks, he felt as though he had already almost succeeded in his enterprise. Dismounting, he listened awhile intently. Then, satisfied that he was alone, he secured the mare, and leaned against one of the three or four ruined columns still standing. He knew he was before the appointed time, but he could not refrain from the hope that Nakhala would be consumed by a feverish impatience equal to his own. Still, the time passed as if it were water oozed drop by drop from an almost closed crevice.

Colonel Le Marchant was a brave man. Nevertheless he was conscious of a thrill of paralysing fear when, out of the silence and the darkness, and apparently from the ground close by, three veiled figures approached. He had heard no one, not even the faintest rustle. For a moment he knew the instinctive dread of the supernatural; then he feared that he was caught in an ambush.

"Eugene!" said a woman's voice — a low thrilling whisper that sent the blood surging from his heart again, and made him take a quick step forward.

"Dolores... Nakhala... I am here!... Who are those with you?"

The girl moved rapidly towards him, and the next moment was in his arms.

"Eugene... Eugene... I love you. Oh that we could escape from those who are jealous of our happiness!"

"So we can, my beautiful Dolores, and at once — now! Who are those with you?"

"But you know how bitter my father is against the French — against all *Roumi* in truth. And —"

"But you are a Spaniard."

"Nay, I am of the Beni-Es-Saära — the People of the Desert."

"But now you are free, Dolores! Come, do not let us linger. Any moment you may be followed, any moment we may be intercepted. Tell me, who are those who —"

"And my father, Eugene, Mahomet El-Djebeli, wishes me to wed Si Suleiman ben Khaddour. What can I do? I cannot be a curse to my own people. There is but one way to happiness, but that is a way you will not take."

"Speak, Nakhala, what is this way?"

"To-morrow, Eugene, Bou-Amama and his followers and prisoners will pass southward. Si Suleiman will join him with a thousand men as soon as Bou-Amama reaches the western and southern shores of the Chott-El-Chergui."

"Do not disturb yourself about Suleiman, Nakhala. I have him in my power."

In the gloom Le Marchant did not see the girl's sudden start, and he was too preoccupied to notice a curious movement in the dark shadow that lay enmassed behind the very column against which he had been leaning.

"You — have — Si Suleiman — in your power?"

"Yes. He is to come to me to-morrow. He will never leave El Khadthera — or, at any rate, not till this war is over and you and I have gone hence. But now, quick, tell me what it is you would have me do?"

"Eugene Le Marchant, if you will keep your troops in garrison to-morrow, I will come to you in the evening. If you will not do this, then you never see me again."

For a moment Colonel Le Marchant did not fully grasp what Nakhala meant. Then the whole thing flashed upon him as if in a sudden flare of light.

"Dolores, you do not know what you ask. If Bou-Amama is making for Géryville he must pass close to us. What will my troops think if they see me allowing an insurgent Arab to give us the slip, a victorious rebel, rich with booty, encumbered with Christian prisoners? The thing is impossible!"

"Then it is as I feared. We must part at once."

"But this is monstrous. You cannot ask me to do this thing, Nakhala."

"It is not I who ask, Eugene. I have no choice. We are snared, you and I, as though we were helpless quails."

"Snared — how snared!"

"My father discovered my flight. On menace of immediate death I confessed that I was hastening to meet you. He gave me the choice, — death, or to win you over. And as the Arabs have done you no harm, it seemed to me that you would not condemn us both to death merely for the sake of molesting Bou-Amama."

"My God, Nakhala, I do not care a grain of sand for Bou-Amama: but duty ... duty ... and, above all, the prisoners ... the unfortunate women! But what do you mean about Mahomet's condemning us both to death?"

"We are surrounded. Ah, do not attempt to use your revolver, — it is too late; a cry from either of these men, and we shall be captives in a moment."

"This is an ambush!"

"Even so; but what could I do, Eugene?"

"We must make an effort to escape. As soon as I fire, leap on my mare. I will fire again, and then leap up beside you. We may even yet get away."

"No, it is too late. We are surrounded, I tell you."

"Well?"

"This: we are to be buried alive beneath two of these great columns."

The next moment Colonel Le Marchant raised his arm. Almost simultaneously a flare of flame and a crashing report came from behind the nearest column. The revolver he had held was blown from his hand, while his arm fell to his side temporarily paralysed.

A profound silence ensued. There were still only Nakhala and the two impassive veiled Arabs. The Colonel was convinced.

"Life ... *your* life ... *our* life, Nakhala ... is at stake. I cannot lose you, Dolores. It may mean ruin to me; but I agree."

"Oh, Eugene, Eugene, you have saved us!"

"Can you not come with me now? I will keep my promise."

"No. It is impossible. To-morrow night without fail, but not to-night."

"Then I suppose I am to go now ... and in safety?"

"Yes. All will now be well. But ... Eugene ... remember! If you break your troth you will not only never see me again, but will be the cause of my ruin, my death."

"I have given my word, Dolores. And see, I accept yours. You say you will come to me to-morrow night. *Voilà:* I believe it."

"*She will come!*"

Le Marchant swung round as he heard the harsh gutteral voice, a voice that seemed vaguely familiar to him. But there was no one visible. He strode forward. A momentary glimpse he caught of a tall figure, then it was lost in the darkness. When he looked round again, Nakhala had disappeared.

He seemed to be absolutely alone. Was it all a dream, he wondered. No: there was the evidence of his shattered revolver, his still aching arm. He had a presentiment of further ill: but of what avail were presentiments? He had made his choice, and must abide by it. There was nothing to be done but to ride back and await the course of events.

Dawn was breaking as he saluted the sentinel at the gate of El Khadthera. He had seen no one on the road, had in no way been molested; yet more than once his strained ears told him that he was not alone on the sandy wilderness which lay between the fort and Sidi Khalifa.

The sentry who passed him did not know which was the whiter: the white dawn that stole above the barren hills and undulating desert, the white body of *Vent-du-Paradis*, or the white face of Colonel Le Marchant.

The morning passed slowly, the noontide more slowly still. The officers of the garrison were seated at *déjeuner* when an orderly entered with the news that a large body of Arab troops was visible to the north-west, apparently coming from Sidi Khalifa and bound southward by the Géryville route.

"It must be Bou-Amama!" cried Major Cazin; "the news must be true about his being on the march south!"

"Now we shall have some fighting!" muttered the junior officers to each other; "and high time too. In a few days more even El Khadthera would be under the spell of that rebel."

Even while the excitement was still novel, further tidings arrived. It was indeed Bou-Amama. He was passing, however, as a victorious captain making a wise movement: not as a defeated warrior in flight. His banners were flying, and in the midst of his irregular following was the Green Standard. The last messenger vowed that Bou-Amama Bel-Arbi openly jeered at the French, telling his still only half convinced army that the French were afraid, and that even the powerful garrison of El Khadthera would not venture to molest him.

By this time not only the officers but the troops were in a state of eager excitement. This became frenzy when yet another messenger came in with confirmation of the news that there were about two hundred European prisoners in Bou-Amama's train, and among them no fewer than sevenscore women and girls.

From where Colonel Le Marchant and his officers stood, on a low mamelon near the western gate of the fort, the rebel Arab army could be seen with ease. To the amazement of all, it was rapidly approaching. A furtive movement became noticeable among the natives crowded along the old grassy rampart to the south of the gate.

"See there, *mon colonel*," said Captain Roussel, significantly: "what does *that* mean?"

"Natural curiosity, I presume," was the response, in a cold hard voice.

"We had better keep an eye on them all the same. It may be a concerted movement. *Ma foi*, it looks as though Bou-Amama were coming within rifle-range! He can't be mad enough to be bent on a show-off, and surely he's not going to try and take the fort at a rush."

"Be so good as to keep your opinions to yourself till they are asked for, Captain Roussel," said Colonel Le Marchant, with sudden anger. His junior regarded him for a moment with a resentful flush, saluted, and stiffly drew back.

Soon there was no longer doubt that Bou-Amama was coming close to El Khadthera. Was it to attempt an assault, or to lure the garrison to issue to open combat, or in sheer bravado?

All eyes were now turned upon the Colonel, who stood fixedly regarding the advancing force, whose derisive cheers and shouts of mockery and defiance were now clearly heard.

At last Major Cazin could restrain himself no longer.

"Shall we open fire, Colonel Le Marchant?"

"No."

"But ... pardon me, *mon colonel* ... Bou-Amama may take the fort by a rush; and the Arabs here — they are already excited enough! If they rose while we were beating back a sudden onrush it might go badly with us."

"Bou-Amama will not attack us, Major Cazin. This is mere bravado on his part."

"But, good heavens, sir, we can't allow this successful rebel to tarnish us with cowardice — to slip past us! Why, with that rag-tag following of his we could send him to the right-about in ten minutes; and if he is fool enough to fight we could pulverize his force, simply pulverise it!"

"*I* am the sole judge of what is best to be done, Major Cazin."

"But, Colonel Le Marchant ... why, my God! ... *mon colonel* — the prisoners! the hundred and fifty women and girls!"

"Well?"

"*Well* ... Colonel, I — I — don't understand," stammered Major Cazin, while those about him looked on with mingled astonishment, anger, and rising shame.

The Colonel turned, and again steadfastly regarded the enemy, whose vanguard was now within five or six hundred yards distance. Suddenly a mounted Arab dashed forward and rode at full speed towards the fort, his burnous streaming in the wind and the sunlight flashing on the barrel of his long rifle as it lay in the hollow of his left arm.

When within fifty yards from the rampart he swerved, and, managing his horse with consummate skill, went slowly caracoling along the whole western front of the fort.

As he rode he shouted alternately in Arabic and French: "Ho there, dogs and sons of dogs! Let every infidel tremble! Bou-Amama laughs at you! He spits in your faces! But he spares you yet a little while. Eat, drink, and be merry while you can, for in a few days he will come again and wipe both you and El Khadthera from the face of the earth. See! he passes, scorning and deriding you! We have slain your comrades like jackals, and the vultures are busy with your young Sheik Weimbrenner!"

Here a deep hoarse growl arose from the French soldiers in the fort, terrible, menacing, like the savage snarl of an infuriated tiger before it leaps against the bars of its cage, and, breaking them, springs upon the fools who taunt him.

"Bou-Amama Bel-Arbi will be compassionate, dogs though ye be!" went on the envoy, in a loud mocking voice, rising to a scream ever and again: "ay, he will have mercy upon you, if you will lay down your arms, and bow down before the great name of the Prophet of Allah! Otherwise he will grind you like dust, he will stamp you under his heel, as the horse stamps the dry dung into the sand, for ye too are carrion — *Djifa — djifa — djifa !*"

The hoarse growl rose now to fierce execrations, savage gripping of rifles, a panting, shuddering breath of murderous fury.

"See! The great Sheik scorns you! He will not go one yard out of his way. We are treading on the skirts of El Khadthera and will rest at Ain Sifi-sifa: will you meet us there? *Pah:* you will not stir from your fort! You do not even dare to fire a shot; though, sheltered as you are, you could slay scores of us with your rifles! No: you are not men, as we Arabs are. Ha! Ha! Ha! That is what your wives and daughters and young women will say! Ha! Ha! Ha! sevenscore goodly women have we carried away to be our slaves and concubines!"

Through the whole force went a shock as though an electric flash had stricken it. The sudden silence, save for a dull sound as of sobbing breath, was full of unspeakable rage, of unutterable menace. The officers on the mamelon looked at their colonel. They could see his face in profile only; but saw that it was ashy white, and that the muscles twitched convulsively.

An expression of consternation came into the faces already hard-set in anger and indignation. Each man looked at his companions, then at the Colonel, then at Major Cazin, then at the Colonel again. Meanwhile, tossing his rifle and catching it on high, flaunting his loose burnous, and making his horse swerve and rear, the Arab champion leisurely retraced his way. But as he went he laughed again and again, now taunting the French with cowardice, now mocking the fate of the unhappy women in the grip of Bou-Amama.

There was the dead silence of intense expectation as Major Cazin strode to the side of his superior officer.

"Colonel Le Marchant, we are ready. Will you give the word of command?"

The Colonel slowly looked round. His features were drawn; his face was of a dull greyish hue.

"For what?"

The voice was dry, harsh, as though the man were dying of thirst.

"For what . . . for what . . . Colonel!" exclaimed Major Cazin, whose eyes gleamed like those of a beast of prey. "You are not going to let the French flag be so grossly insulted! you are not going to make every man of the garrison drink the bitterest cup of shame a Frenchman has ever been asked to drink! Good God, sir, you are not going to stand by while that devil Bou-Amama marches by unmolested and takes with him two hundred of our kith and kin, a hundred and forty wives and maidens!"

"I have my orders," was the reply in a low voice, yet not so low but that every officer heard it, and, hearing, flushed with bitter shame and wrath.

"We know your orders, Colonel Le Marchant. But no orders could stand in the way of our present duty. We will be for ever disgraced in the eyes of the Arabs, of our comrades in North Africa, of our nation, of our enemies, of the whole world, if we do not at once sally forth. There is not a man of us who would not gladly die to avert this stain on the honour of France!"

"Major Cazin, you forget yourself. I, and I alone, have the right to decide what is our duty. I will not argue the matter with you; but be so good as to understand that, while we shall defend ourselves from actual attack, I will not meanwhile engage in battle with Bou-Amama."

"But, sir, *mon colonel*, the women — the prisoners!"

"I have spoken."

A look of fierce contempt came into every face. One sentiment pervaded the whole force, officers and men: their colonel was afraid!

Major Cazin did not bow. At first he made no sign, no movement, though a strange purplish tinge spread from his lips to his cheeks. When he did speak every one heard, and with indrawn breath awaited the answer.

"Colonel Le Marchant, as an officer of the

Army of the Republic, I protest. As a soldier of France, I curse this hour of shame. Even now, will you save us this disgrace?"

There was no answer. A tremulous movement was visible in the Colonel's ashy face.

"Eugene Le Marchant, you are a coward!"

The suspense was terrible. After this insult, this gross dereliction from duty, even the most long suffering man must turn.

Colonel Le Marchant veered slowly. With a mechanical gesture he pointed westward:

"See: the enemy is now in full retreat."

But, save for a momentary glance, no one looked at the enemy.

"Major Cazin!"

"Sir!"

"Give me your sword. I place you under arrest. You will answer for this revolt, for this insult, at a court where your bravado will be of no avail."

"Colonel Le Marchant, it is you who fear me, not I who fear what you can do. See, here is my sword, but, lest it should ever be said that Lucien Cazin surrendered his sword to a coward and traitor, I break it across my knee."

As he spoke, Major Cazin suited his action to his words. Then, flinging the splintered weapon on the ground, he turned abruptly on his heel and walked away.

With a slow step Colonel Le Marchant followed. As he passed the group of officers, not one saluted.

The afternoon went past in a gloom full of sullen wrath and menace. The soldiers talked of nothing but the Colonel's cowardice, Major Cazin's insult, Bou-Amama's insolent triumph, the fate of the prisoners, the events of the morrow, the outcome of the inevitable court-martial.

In his room, sitting with his bowed head in his hands, Eugene Le Marchant thought only of Nakhala.

"It is for you, Dolores! It is for you!" he kept muttering over and over.

A sudden blare of a bugle broke the stillness. It was sundown. The Colonel rose, went out into the wide sandy road, and walked swiftly towards the south gate.

A little group was clustered round the sentry on duty. It gave way as the Colonel approached. The first person he recognised was Abdallah: but blind, newly mutilated.

On the ground before the renegade Arab was a figure clad in a long white robe. Colonel Le Marchant noticed how ghastly white it looked with the long black hair streaming across it like a flood of ink.

"Where is the Sheik of El Khadthera," Abdallah was crying in Arabic over and over in a strained hysterical voice.

"Here."

"Ah, it is you," said the mutilated wretch, gasping in his excitement. "I come from Si Suleiman ben Khaddour. It was he who took me before Bou-Amama; it was he who at the Sheik's order did *this*"—and as he spoke he pointed with shaking hand at his ember-bleared eyes.

"What do you want with me; what is your message?" interrupted Colonel Le Marchant stonily, with his eyes fixed on the white figure lying so inertly upon the ground, the white figure with the long black hair streaming across it.

"Before I was sent hence I was summoned before Bou-Amama, Si Suleiman, and Mahomet El-Djebeli. They bade me tell you that the Children of the Desert always keep their pledges. Nakhala, the adopted daughter of the Blind Sheik, promised to be with you this evening. So, she has kept her pledge. But I have a message to give you along with this dead woman."

"What?"

Colonel Le Marchant spoke as if unconcernedly. His eyes were still on the motionless white figure, but he seemed to regard with little save curiosity what he knew to be the corpse of his beautiful Dolores.

"Si Suleiman said to me: 'Tell the French Sheik, Le Marchant, that I send my wife Nakhala to keep her tryst with him. Tell him that as she was mine in life, he is welcome to her in death.'"

Colonel Le Marchant stooped, lifted back the burnous from the corpse, and looked for a few seconds at the beautiful face.

"Let her be buried according to the rites of the Catholic Church," he said simply, and then walked back to his quarters.

On his way he met and stopped the senior captain.

"Captain Roussel, I have just received instructions to pursue Bou-Amama and prevent his taking and fortifying Géryville. Si Suleiman ben Khaddour has at last seceded to the rebels. We must march at once. You will act in place of Major Cazin."

Captain Roussel drew himself up stiffly, saluted, and, with an ill-disguised look of contempt, turned to give the necessary orders.

A VENETIAN IDYL.

A Venetian Idyl.

———◆———

THEY are pleasant rooms, those which my friend and I shared in Venice early last summer. Situate as they are at the eastern extremity of the Traghetto San Gregorio, the windows to the front look out on all the life and beauty of the Grand Canal, though the house itself is entered by a closed courtyard opening off the quiet Rio. It is true that not infrequently in the evenings loud voices and laughter and shrill cries are heard; for, as the name discloses, the Traghetto is one of those stations where gondoliers await their customers, and any one who has lived in Venice will realise at once that the poetic silence universally supposed to characterise the widowed queen of the Adriatic is a hollow delusion if, in the neighbourhood, there be a gondola station. The men have a habit, also, convenient for themselves, but hardly so agreeable to inoffensive outsiders ignorant even of the cause of dispute, of quarrelling from opposite banks of a canal, whence any amount of ferocious vituperation can be hurled with perfect safety — the common methods by which nearly all disputes in Venice are settled. But, after all, such occasional noisiness is more than balanced by the otherwise delightful situation. Almost since the day of our arrival in the ever-new and ever-beautiful city, we had employed the same gondolier, by name Alessandro Luigi Tremazzi (as we afterwards learned, for at first he was known to us only by his familiar appellation Luigi), and had ultimately engaged his exclusive services for a month at the moderate rate of four and a half lire a day.

It was this Luigi who, early one morning, towards the end of last May, brought us our coffee and asked what were the immediate orders of the Signori. We had felt, even before perceiving the fact, that a scirocco was blowing; and before Luigi's advent we had debated for some time whether to spend the first part of the day with Tintoretto and Titian, or to sail northward to Torcello, so as, on our return, to see Venice and the lagoons in the beautiful silver-and-amethyst veil of a scirocco sunset. We had decided on the latter course; so, having given the needful orders, we despatched our rolls and coffee and fruit. We before long found ourselves installed in the roomy gondola which we had told Luigi to direct first to the Lido, so that we might have a swim before starting in earnest on our journey. As we passed San Giorgio on the right, and found the Lion of St. Mark's and the Doge's Palace on our left giving place to the busy Riva degli Schiavoni, we noticed that the little wind there was seemed to be decreasing, so much so as to promise to fail altogether ere long. We determined, therefore, to wait till after our bathe before deciding finally as to Torcello; for we could not in fairness ask Luigi to take us such a distance during the prostrating and thundery heat of a windless scirocco day.

As we neared Sant' Elisabetta (or "the Lido," as this part of the Lido of Malamacco is now, even by the Venetians themselves, invariably called) the flagging breeze regained a little of its energy; and though neither the sky above nor the lagoon beneath had anything of that wonderful azure transparency so characteristic of them at most other times, yet they had a delicate pale blue that was almost as lovely. Right alongside the gondola, indeed, the water had a dull greenish hue, chiefly imparted to it by the masses of green trailing sea-hair which the morning tide waved up from the shallow depths.

Leaving Luigi and our boat in the little harbour, we strolled across the island, and in ten minutes felt the sea-wind on our faces, and saw before us the Adriatic sparkling away into seemingly illimitable distance, leagues beyond leagues of moving blue, relieved only by a white crest here and there, a snowy gull sweeping suddenly in its flight, and some half-dozen widely dispersed fishing-boats endeavouring to make the most of the wind that, at intervals, puffed out their orange, brick-red, or saffron-hued sails.

Endlessly beautiful as was this view, we soon deserted it for the Stabilimento, whence, after a long and delightful swim in the salt and buoyant waves, we joined Luigi: for we had noticed a deepening of the blue to the south, and were now intent upon reaching Torcello. As we passed the green promontory of the Public Gardens we heard the gondolier make some remark about the weather, but his meaning escaped us, and it was not till we were close upon San Michele that he spoke again. Beyond this island graveyard an exquisite silveriness permeated the already hazy atmosphere to the north and west, till at last it seemed as if a veil of thinnest gossamer had been invisibly spun from below and above, an aerially transparent veil that caused every distant object or outline upon which we looked to seem as though beheld in a mirage. In what might have been mere dreamland vision, we saw, thus, the Venetian district of Canarreggio and the dim islands of the lagoons to the south of Mestre; and even adjacent Murano lost some of its unsightliness, and gleamed as a great, dusky nectarine on a sunside wall. But while we were silently watching this visible scirocco-breath, we heard Luigi's second interruption, a politely-worded hint that it would not be an agreeable day for the signori to proceed to Torcello. On asking him wherefore, he told us that it would be exceptionally close and thundery till the afternoon, and that then a storm of more or less severity would probably break. Knowing from experience how weather-wise our gondolier was, we at once relinquished our project: and straightway agreed to return homeward, to disembark at San Nicoletto, and have our luncheon and afternoon smoke under the shadowy acacias at that most beautiful, though least known, part of the Lido. An hour later, then, we were sitting in the cool and exquisitely fragrant acacia shade, and by no means disappointed at the enforced change in our plans. While lazily smoking after our light luncheon, and as lazily looking out upon the metallic grey-blue of the lagoons beyond us, or listening to the humming of the wild bees among the innumerable white clusters overhead, one of us asked Luigi to tell us a story, true or legendary, as he preferred. Our gondolier himself looked the hero of some Venetian romance. Tall and strong, but lithe rather than largely built, with wavy masses of black hair curling over his sun-tanned forehead and down upon his brown neck; with dark grey eyes that were at once indolent and fiery in their expression; and with a pleasant smile lingering always about his mouth; he bore his thirty years so well, and with such unconscious grace, that neither painter nor romancist could have found a better model amongst the gondoliers of Venice or the fisherfolk of Chioggia.

Laughingly he replied to our request, that he could sing the songs of his craft, but that he was not a good story-teller, and, moreover, that he remembered nothing that could interest the Signori. But when my friend suggested to him that he should tell us something about himself, if this were not asking too much, he blushed slightly as though with gratified pleasure, adding immediately that, if it would please us to hear, he would tell us how he won and married the pretty wife whom he had taken us to visit the other day.

Throwing himself in an easy posture in the acacia shade beside us, Luigi remained silent for a few moments, and then began in his soft and sibilant Venetian the following narration, which, however, does not pretend to follow with exactness his own phraseology.

"I don't think the heroes of stories, even in stories related by the chief actors themselves, are possessed of only one name. So, though to every one I am known only as Luigi, I may begin by saying that I am the only son of my dead father Giovan' Andrea, and that my own name in full is Alessandro Luigi Tremazzi. I was christened Alessandro after my father's father, and Luigi after my maternal grandfather, but was always called by the former name until my sixth or seventh year, when my father began invariably to address me as Luigi, — a change that I afterwards discovered to be due to an act of shameful treachery on the part of his bosom friend, Alessandro Dà Ru, after whom I had been named in common with my father's father. I mention this only because Dà Ru's son, Matteo, with whom my father forbade me ever to play or even to speak, turns up again in my narrative, and there's always more than one traitor in a traitor's nest. However, things went on with us, sometimes well and sometimes ill, till my twenty-fifth year. At this time my father owned two gondolas, one quite new, and the other considerably dilapidated by many years' use; and as strangers generally prefer a young and active to an old man it generally happened that I took up my station at the Piazzetta with the new gondola, while my father did ferry or 'barca' duty with the other at a Traghetto near the Rio di S. Vito, opposite the Giudecca. Between us we managed to get along without getting into debt. Owing, however, to the old man's mania for investing his money in lotteries and other speculations of like uncertainty, it was little that, even in the busy spring and autumn seasons, we were able to put aside, and this little certainly never survived a winter. If the money had not gone in this fashion we should have been very well-to-do indeed: for at an average of from six to eight lire a day between us throughout the year, we should have been better off than nine out of every ten of our neighbours, having no one to share or depend upon our profits. About this time my father died, the doctor saying it was from eating too much ripe melon, and the parish priest declaring that it was a sign of divine displeasure at old Tremazzi's not having been to mass for a year come Corpus Christi. My father had been a rather hard and taciturn man, but I missed him sorely at first; however, the poor must work however much they grieve, and, moreover, my life had just become filled with a new and absorbing interest. For some weeks before my father's death I had regularly gone every leisure half-hour to a small café on the Riva degli Schiavoni: not because I specially wanted either coffee or iced orange-water, but because it was next door to the tiny rope-shop of old Salvatore Agujani. You may be sure I did not spend my *soldi* at the café merely to look at the interior of a rope-seller's shop, nor even for the pleasure of occasionally conversing a little with white-haired Salvatore himself. But Signor Agujani had a grand-daughter who lived with him, and who frequently was to be seen in the little shop itself.

"It is not for me, Signori, to say too much about the beauty of 'La Biondina,' as many of the neighbours called her, considering that she is now my wife: but you have seen her yourselves, and can therefore judge if she does not deserve to be known as 'Zena la Bionda.' You saw how golden-fair her hair is, how dark blue are her eyes, how white her beautiful neck and delicate hands, how joyous is her laughter; but you can't guess how much fairer she seems to me when I come home at nights for my fried fish and macaroni, to see her sitting beside me and laughing at our baby's frantic efforts to reach me. But I am getting on too fast, and giving you the sequel before I have done with the beginning.

"When my father was buried yonder in San Michele, I found myself possessor of the two boats. I sold the old one, almost useless as a gondola, to an acquaintance who was content to get through life with such profits as the ownership of a 'barca' could bring in. With the proceeds, and what little money there was lying by, I paid off all debts, and began the world on my own account with my nearly new gondola, which I rechristened 'La Biondina.'

"By this time, I ought to say, there was an unworded understanding between Zena and myself. How well I remember the day when I first took her to see the change in my boat's name! It was the Festa of Corpus Christi, and I had determined on two things when I rose at sunrise: firstly, that I should keep the day as a holiday; secondly, that, if possible, I should get a definite answer from Zena, whether for good or ill, before I lay down to rest again. Punctually at seven o'clock I was at the Riva degli Schiavoni, wishing good morning to old Salvatore; and, at that very moment, Zena came out, looking lovelier than any flower you can see here on the Lido. Then the three of us went off to the Piazza to see the grand procession, and to get blessed by the Cardinal Archbishop in St. Mark's. Throughout the rest of the day we met and talked with acquaintances, and idled and ate ices like the rich *forestieri* themselves. After sundown, when all Venice that could afford it was on the water, every one eager to see the hundreds of gondolas flitting to and fro upon the Grand Canal, or clustering by the score round the huge illuminated barge filled with musicians. Then, too, there were the beautiful fireworks shooting up endlessly all along the banks, from the end of the Schiavoni to the Rialto and the station at the extreme northwest.

We, too, went out on the canal in my gondola, — for though I could have let it that evening for so large a sum as ten lire, I swear that fifty lire would not have made me forego the pleasure of taking Zena out to see the end of the great Festa. As we came along the Piazzetta, her grandfather turned to speak to some friend: so I had time to take her down to the boat itself, and managed to swing the prow aside, so as to show Zena the name freshly painted on the narrow bulwark. When she saw 'La Biondina' written there she blushed as red as a rose, and then asked me coquettishly what had made me change its name from 'La Bella Esperanza;' whereupon I replied that to own 'La Biondina' *was* my 'Bella Esperanza;' and here she blushed again more deeply than before. Knowing I might not have another opportunity that night, I stooped forward and whispered, 'Zena, *carissima*, I love you with all my heart; do you think you will ever love me enough in return to be my wife?' and to my delight and joy she breathed rather than said, 'I have loved you always, Luigi.' Ah! the happiness of that night! I shall never forget it; and, you may be sure, Signori, that we looked more at one another than at the fireworks or the innumerable gondolas filled with gayly dressed *forestieri*, and listened more eagerly to each other's lightest word than to the music which continuously was swept up and down the Grand Canal by the soft night wind. I said to myself that it seemed all too good to be true, but I little guessed that my light thought was to be followed by a sad reality.

"I said nothing that night to old Agujani; and even when I parted with Zena nought passed between us but an ardent hand-pressure and a loving glance into each other's eyes. After my return home I could not sleep for a long time, because of my great happiness. At last, however, I fell into a sound doze; though not a dreamless one, for twice ere morning I dreamt that I was a little boy once more, and that my father was telling me never again to play or speak with Matteo, the son of Alessandro Dà Ru, adding the proverb I had so often heard him muttering between his teeth, 'There's always more than one traitor in a traitor's nest.'

"When I woke it was with such lightness of heart as I suppose the larks have on a cloudless April morning. Before mid-day, however, all my joy had vanished, or at any rate had been sorely damped; for, you must know, I was officially informed that I was a navy conscript. In other words, notice was given me that I must without delay join one of the King's ships of war for a term of three years. As you may imagine, this was a sad blow to my ardent hopes. I had no way of escape; firstly, because I had no mother or children dependent on me and was also in good health; and secondly, because I could not afford to pay for a substitute, even if the authorities should permit my doing so. There was nothing for it but to store up my gondola for the three years, or else to sell it, and then to settle matters and depart. This does n't, perhaps, seem much to do, and of course many of my friends and acquaintances have undergone similar experiences; yet I can tell you my heart was sore indeed when I broke the news to poor Zena. She took it bravely, however, and assured me with tears in her eyes that three years would soon pass; that she would write often, and that she would never swerve from her pledged fealty to me. Also she persuaded me to say nothing about our engagement to her grandfather, because the latter would be sure to object to her being bound down through three years of absence on my part.

"Well, Signori, I need not dwell upon what were sad enough days to Zena and myself, but the long and short of it is that in less than a week after the official intimation I was on board the 'Ré Umberto.' You may be sure Livorno seemed a poor enough place to me after Venice, and that the life of a man-of-war's man was anything but a welcome exchange from the honourable freedom of a gondolier, — a gondolier, moreover, who owned his boat. But I mustn't weary you with details as to how these three years went by, save that sometimes we were stationed at Livorno, sometimes at Spezzia, again at Tunis or at Alexandria, but never once at Venice. On one occasion my heart beat high when I heard it rumoured that the 'Ré Umberto' had been ordered to Trieste, for then I knew that if I could get a couple of days' leave I should be able to get across to Venice and have a glimpse of my sweetheart; however, nothing came of this rumour, and when we left Corfu we steered south-westward and not towards the north.

"I should have told you before this that, when I joined my ship, I found two or three acquaintances amongst the conscripts, but on the night of my arrival only one known face met my gaze, — the face of Matteo Dà Ru. I had seen little or nothing of my former playmate for several years past, as old Dà Ru had left his home in the Giudecca some five years before my father's death and joined the fishing fraternity at Chioggia, which, as you know, Signori, is some thirty miles to the south of this. Distance as well as local prejudices continue to keep the inhabitants of the northern and southern lagoons apart: and even, as in the Giudecca itself, intermarriage with a man or woman of the town proper is not approved of. But though Matteo and I had met seldom of recent years, we knew each other well, and I could not but have a kindly feeling to an acquaintance encountered under such circumstances, — one, moreover, whom I had known since we were little boys together. Yet, curiously enough, I experienced what was nearly a feeling of repulsion when we embraced one another with friendly salutations, — just as if I heard again my old father telling me to have nothing to do with kith or kin of Alessandro Dà Ru, and muttering his proverb about traitors. Although I guessed by this time what it was that had come between my father and his friend, I no longer thought it fitting I should renounce the latter's son for a crime of which he was wholly guiltless; and so it was that, although we never became friends in the true sense of the word, we learnt to like each other well enough to be decidedly friendly acquaintances.

"All this time, of course, I heard at more or less regular intervals from Zena, — letters always welcome, because they told me she was well and happy. It is true these letters were not written by herself. Yet though the penmanship was that of old Antonio Baruccio, the public letter-writer who sits at the right-hand corner of the Campo di Santa Maria Formoso, to me they were the same as though she had written them, partly because I knew the words were hers, and partly because, I am ashamed to say, I could n't at that time read handwriting myself. I may say now, Signori, that both Zena and myself not only read but write fairly well; but at the time I am speaking of I had always to call in assistance to get through my sweetheart's notes, and to indite my own in return. I had found a trustworthy confidant in Gian' Battista, the boatswain's mate, and during the greater part of my time this good friend acted the part of reader and secretary for me, and never once betrayed my sweetheart's name to my comrades. About three months before the close of my time, we were stationed at Spezzia: and while there I, in common with Matteo Dà Ru and half-a-dozen others, was drafted off to the gunboat 'La Fiamma,' as the crew of the latter required reinforcement owing to the extra trouble smugglers from the French and North African coasts had given of late. There had for more than a year past been a growing coolness between Matteo and myself, — a coolness that had arisen without any definite cause, but strong enough to prevent my making him a confidant in my affairs and hopes. But one night, when we were together in the same watch, I determined to tell him about Zena and myself, having so resolved on account of my friend Gian' Battista being no longer at hand to help me with my correspondence. I knew, too, that I ought soon to hear from Venice, as I had sent a letter there soon after we arrived in the Gulf of Spezzia. For four months past I had had no news of my sweetheart. I knew this was no fault of hers, as

I felt certain she had written to such addresses as I had given her before the sudden departure of the 'Umberto' for the west. During this period we had been to Monte Video, returning by the coasts of Morocco, and finally by those of Algeria and Tunis: and it was not surprising that Zena's letters should have persistently wandered astray among such widely apart places as Corfu, Alexandria, Messina, Gibraltar, Monte Video, and the North African stations. None the less I was eager for even a scrap of news, and longed till another day should bring me the reply to my last letter. By this time I could read a little, though only slowly and with difficulty; yet I hoped to make out Zena's letter by myself, or at any rate to do so after it had once been read over to me by a friend.

"In an emergency one cannot always be particular, and thus it was I came to confide in Matteo. As I said, we were one evening together in the same watch; we had been talking about our term, which would shortly expire, and about what we would do when we got our final discharge.

"'My father would like me to join him in

his fishery business at Chioggia,' said Matteo; 'but I have no intention of doing so. I have my gondola safely stored up, and will try to get my old place at the Piazzetta again. Then perhaps I will get a wife, and have a comfortable home, after all this jumbling about in the western seas.'

"'Oh, then,' I replied, 'you are thinking of marrying, are you? Come, come, my friend, a man doesn't generally think that in earnest unless he has some one in view. Why did you never say anything of this to me before?'

"'For the same reason, I suppose,' answered Matteo, 'that you never confided in me. Do you think I am blind, that I never saw you writing letters (or rather getting Gian' Battista to do them for you) whenever we were anywhere in port? I knew your father was dead, and I didn't suppose you wrote so often to Francesco, or Tito, or Paolo, or any other of our fellow-gondoliers.'

"'Tell me this, then,' I said laughingly; 'is your sweetheart dark or fair? Mine is as fair as a May day is to a December night. I'll swear she is the most beautiful *biondina* in all Italy.'

"'Is she so very fair,' asked Matteo, with sudden eagerness — 'is she so very fair? I'll lay you a day's wage, *cam'rado mio*, that she is not the equal of the girl I love! Come, tell me her name, and it may be that some friend here knows the girls, and so can decide as to which is the fairer.'

"'No, no,' I said, 'I asked you first. Tell me the name of your sweetheart, and I'll tell you mine.'

"'Not so; but if you like, we'll toss for it. "Heads" to tell first.'

"'Agreed!'

"Whereupon Matteo flung six *soldi* into the air, four of which came down 'heads' upward, so that it was I who had to disclose my secret first.

"'*Altro!* she is called La Biondina, because she is so fair and beautiful, by those who know her well; Zena la Bionda, by others; and Signorina Zena Agujani by strangers and customers who call at her grandfather's shop in the Riva degli Schiavoni. *Ecco, la mia biondina!*'

"Just then I heard the officer of the watch call out something sharply to some one forward, and turned my head to listen; but, hearing no sound of any kind from Matteo, I looked round again, and was startled to see his face ghastly pale and his dead-black eyes glittering with what looked to me like uncontrolled hate.

"'What's the matter, Matteo,' I cried, 'and why do you look at me thus?'

"He did not reply at first, but kept his eyes fixed on me with the same strange expression; then he stammered something about not feeling well, and that I was to take no notice of it. He said it was a return of the same complaint he used to suffer from occasionally after being out most of the night with the fishing-boats, a kind of cramp in the stomach. This fully accounted to me for his ghastly look, though at first I had been startled into vague alarm.

"'Are you better now?' I asked; but before he answered he stepped closer into the dark shadow that stretched between us and the foremast, just as though he were anxious that I should not again see his face. If this was his intention he succeeded; for all I discerned was the dim outline of his figure. It was one of those moonless nights when even the light of the stars seems only sufficient to let us know how dark it is.

"'Yes, yes; I am all right now. And have you been engaged to Zena Agujani all this time? Has she promised to marry you, or is there simply an understanding between you? Does old Salvatore know how matters stand?'

"'One question at a time, my friend,' I said; 'besides, you forget you have not yet fulfilled your part of the agreement. What is the name of your *bella bionda;* is she of Venice or Chioggia?'

"'Oh, I was only joking, Luigi. I was in love for a time with a golden-haired girl from Trieste, who lived with her uncle at Fusina; but she had too fiery a tongue for me, and the last I heard of her was that she had married Piero Carelli, the lemon merchant at Mestre. I don't believe in blondes, *amico mio;* I never yet heard of one who was true to both lover and husband. Only a dark girl is always true to her lover.'

"'And is that so, Matteo? or is your opinion not based on the simple fact of your sweetheart's having preferred good-tempered Piero

Carelli to a somewhat surly Chioggian fisherman?'

"I had been foolishly provoked at Matteo's remarks about *blondes* in general, and I fully expected my answering sneer would have roused his quick and passionate temper. To my surprise he replied with unexpected eagerness, —

"'Come, Luigi *caro*, don't let us quarrel about a trifle. Here's all health and long life and prosperity to you and your Zena!'

"'You must surely know her by sight,' I said to Matteo; 'for there's hardly a gondolier on the Riva who wouldn't know whom you meant by *La Biondina.*'

"He didn't reply for a moment or two, and when he spoke it was in a somewhat strained voice, —

"'Yes, I know whom you mean. She is beautiful, without doubt. But I'm not on speaking terms with old Salvatore, for some five or six years ago he used language in public about my father for which I have never forgiven him. He may thank his grey hairs he hasn't had the feel of a knife between his ribs before this.'

"I knew this was dangerous ground, so I

began at once to talk about the delights of getting away from shipboard, and of being free once more. Before long our watch was up, and I, at any rate, was not long in falling fast asleep. For some reason I can't explain, my first thought, when I awoke, was connected with what Matteo had been saying about blondes. I laughed at myself for my folly; but do what I would, a vague uneasiness took possession of me, and I began to think that it was, after all, very strange I had not heard from Zena for so long. I remembered now, what I had merely chuckled at in my sleeve before: that, in the last letter I had received, my sweetheart had mentioned her grandfather's having urged her to marry Filippo Faccioli, a middle-aged and very well-to-do ship-chandler, who had a flourishing business on the Fondamenta del Ponte Luongo, in the Giudecca, and who had offered, in a conversation with old Salvatore, to take her with or without dowry. The moment this recollection flashed across my mind I indignantly put it aside again, as I knew Zena too well to suppose she would marry any man, however rich, while she loved another. Nevertheless, I felt uncomfortable all day, all the more as the expected letter had not arrived. In the afternoon I was down below, mending some clothes, and did not notice a government cutter come alongside; but in less than half an hour thereafter I heard the word 'letters' spoken by some one, and you may imagine I bundled up quick enough. Most of the letters had been distributed by the time I got to the quarter-deck; but at last my name was called out, and I stepped forward and received my precious note, retiring with it at once to the quietest spot I could find.

"I had not till then realised how much Matteo's malicious sneer had affected me. The reaction of a glad certainty was so great that the tears were in my eyes, and my hands trembled as I opened the envelope. At this moment I heard Matteo's voice behind me whispering, 'Well, good news, I hope?' and on the impulse I handed the note to him, begging him to read it out to me, as I couldn't spell through it quick enough for my impatience. He took it without a word, and began, 'Dear Luigi,' and then abruptly stopped, and seemed to be glancing through the rest of the letter.

"'Well,' said I, 'seeing that that letter is addressed to me, I think you might as well read it aloud instead of perusing it from beginning to end by yourself.'

"'Don't be angry, Luigi *caro*,' he replied; 'there is bad news in it, old friend, I am sorry to say.'

"'In Heaven's name what is it?' I cried out, with sudden pain. 'Is there anything wrong with Zena?'

"'Do you remember my idle words about blondes last night?' Matteo replied, in a quick low tone; and then, seeing the expression of agony I felt must be in my face, he added, 'See, *caro* Luigi, a lance-thrust is a painful thing, but it is better than the setting-in of a disease; be a man, and bear what many another has had to bear before you. I'll read you the girl's note:—

"'DEAR LUIGI,—I know this letter will bring you a great disappointment. I wouldn't have minded it so much if I thought you had consoled yourself for my absence in any of the ports you have been visiting; but as you swear in your last letter that you have been true to me all along, I believe you.

"'It's not my fault, Luigi, that a rich neighbour

has fallen in love with me, but such is the case, and my grandfather has insisted on my accepting him. He told me that he had lost everything in the world by an unfortunate speculation, and that if not for my own sake, at least for his, I must not refuse this splendid chance. I did n't tell him I expected you home again before long, as this would just have irritated him to no good end. And to be quite honest, Luigi, I must tell you that for some time past I have doubted if I were fitted for you, and if we should be happy. I am afraid not, and this gives me more courage in writing to tell you that, before you receive this letter, I shall be married to our rich neighbour, whose name I will not give you, in case you should curse him in your anger.

"' Try to forgive me, dear Luigi, and believe that I am acting for the best.

"' Still your friend, I sign myself for the last time,
"' Zena Agujani.'

"While this letter was being read to me I felt as if the vessel was sinking under my feet, and then as if every drop in my body was surging round my heart or throbbing in my temples. A blind flood of fury suddenly overcame me, and snatching the letter from Matteo's hands I cursed Zena as a heartless jilt and hypocrite. After that, I rushed away to the foc's'le, where

I threw myself upon my back, to spend the most agonising hours I had ever experienced.

"After what seemed to me weeks of misery I rose, and with trembling hands wrote out in my crabbed letters the following brief note:—

"'To Zena Agujani,—You will never hear from me again.
"'Luigi Tremazzi.'"

"This I likewise myself addressed to 'La gentilezza signorina Zena Agujani, al'casa del Signor Salvatore Agujani, Riva degli Schiavoni, 13½, Venezia.'

"Next morning this letter went on its way; and as I saw the post-bag handed over the side of the 'Fiamma' I felt as if all the happiness of my life went with it also.

"But before I was summoned again on deck for my watch, a sudden suspicion about Matteo flashed across my mind. His conduct was strange the night before, and even during the agony of hearing Zena's letter read, I remembered noting that a peculiar expression, almost of mocking triumph, gleamed upon my comrade's face. Quick as thought I pulled out the letter and slowly spelt it out; but every word from

'Dear Luigi' down to 'Zena Agujani' was just as Matteo had read. My suspicion vanished almost as swiftly as it had arisen, and when I went on deck I was able to disguise the utterance of my misery even from him. Before we turned in again, I told him that of course everything was over between Zena and myself, and that the one request of him I had to make was that he was never to mention her name to me again.

"'I promise,' he said; 'but first let me ask you if you have destroyed her letter. I would if I were you. You'll never forget her treachery as long as you have it with you.'

"When I told him that I had not and did not mean to destroy the letter, I saw him biting his lips as though repressing some hasty exclamation; but he said no more, then or later. Before coming on deck I had buried the cruel note at the bottom of my box, because, though I would not destroy it, I could not bear to carry it about with me. I slept little during that night, and as the dim morning light began to steal in, I lay with half-closed eyes, drowsily thinking of my ruined hopes and of my acute misery. While thus thinking, my eyes, unconsciously to myself, kept watching one of my comrades, who seemed to be looking for his clothes, near where my own were laid. The man suddenly looked up, and instinctively I almost wholly closed my eyes. In a few moments I opened them again, and perceived that the man was Matteo, and that he was feeling in the pockets not of his own clothes but of mine. Something in his stealthy movements made me suspicious. After a moment's hesitation, I sprang from my bunk and asked him what he was doing with my things. I noticed that his first instinct was to snatch the knife from the belt that lay alongside; but the next moment he turned and stammered out,—

"'What do you mean?' adding immediately, 'Oh, I beg your pardon; I see these are your things; I thought they were mine; I wanted to get out a piece of 'baccy I left in one of the pockets last night.'

"With that he turned away at once; and though I could say nothing more, it struck me as strange that any one innocent of any underhand transaction should have been so startled, and should have stammered out so vague excuses with so white a face. Even then it struck me that Matteo, if nothing worse, must surely be a coward.

"Well, Signori, time went by, and at last the day came when a lot of us got our official discharge, duly signed and attested, and were allowed to get ashore at Spezzia, free men once more, Matteo and myself being among this fortunate band.

"*Ecco!* The great day had come at last; but instead of being overcome with joy, I wandered about the little town and along the shores of the bay, sobbing every now and again with my bitter disappointment. I felt half inclined to volunteer to go to sea again, and it was considerably past midnight before I decided to return to Venice; but on inquiry I discovered that the night train for Pisa and Florence had gone, and that I should have to wait some hours. Even miserable hours — which the good God keep from you, Signori — pass somehow, and in due time I found myself at Pisa, then at Bologna, and finally in the mail-train for Venice. I heard some one in the carriage saying he wished he could have left Florence the day before, so as to have spent the whole of Corpus Christi with his friends, and by that

I knew that this day of miserable return was the great Festa, the same on which, three years ago, I had asked Zena to plight me her troth. Well, Signori, to make a short ending to what I'm afraid has been overlong a story, I arrived once more in Venice, between four and five in the afternoon, on the day of Corpus Christi. A sudden fancy took me when I got out at this station. Instead of going to look out for a room for myself, I left my box at the station, and, having jumped into a gondola, told its owner to row me to the Fondamenta del Ponte Luongo, on the Giudecca. When the gondola slid alongside a deserted-looking Traghetto, I told the man to wait, and then walked slowly along the bank till I came to the shop of Faccioli, the ship-chandler, whom I had never doubted to be the man who had stolen my love away from me. While standing near the house and casting sidelong glances up at its windows, a cripple hobbled up to me and begged for a *soldo* in the Virgin's name; but before paying any heed to his request I asked him (though I knew it well) who lived in the house beside us.

"'Why, Signor Faccioli, of course, the rich ship-chandler.'

"'Ah!' I added, 'then I suppose you often see him and his signora come in and out?'

"'You are thinking of the wrong man, signor captain,' replied the cripple, obsequiously; 'the excellent Filippo Faccioli has no wife, though report has it that he wanted to marry a golden-haired child, who is grand-daughter to old Salvatore Agujani, who is a —'

"Without waiting to hear any more I flung a half-dozen *soldi* to the astonished beggar, and, as soon as I had regained the boat, told the gondolier to take me over at once to the Riva degli Schiavoni. As we shot along the wide lagoon, with the Dogana di Mare on the left and the Isle of St. George on the right, a hundred different thoughts coursed through my mind. If Zena hadn't married Signor Faccioli, whom *had* she married? or was she married at all? or was it that death had prevented her from wedding wealthy Filippo? Or had she jilted him even as she had done me? And so on, over and over again.

"When I landed near the Piazzetta, I walked straight toward the well-known little shop. Just as I neared it, I met an acquaintance, who told me (after some inquiries about myself which

I was forced to answer) that he had that moment seen old Agujani on the Piazza listening to the band which was amusing every one till it was dark enough for the fireworks and the water-music to begin. I asked him as calmly as I could if 'La Biondina' was with her grandfather, and he replied he felt sure she was; 'for you don't catch a pretty girl staying at home on the eve of Corpus Christi.'

"I left him then, and his assurances having given me courage, I went up right to the door of the old shop. I don't know why I wanted to see it again, but anyway I did so want; nor do I know why it was I didn't think the door would in all probability be locked, but here again I didn't think anything of the kind. With my heart in my mouth, so to speak, I turned the handle and looked in. Some one looked up and uttered a short cry. It was Zena.

"The next moment she was in my arms, sobbing and kissing me by turns, and I doing pretty much the same thing. Before a happy minute was out, however, she sprang back from me, and, with tears still glittering in her eyes, asked me suddenly what I meant by writing that she would never hear from me again.

"'Here I've been sobbing my life away because of your cruel message! What does it mean, Luigi? Tell me at once — are you married — have you promised any other girl? What is it? — tell me quick!'

"I stammered out, 'Why, look here, Zena, it's I that want to know what you mean by writing me such a horrible letter?'

"'What letter?' she asked in evident surprise.

"'This one,' I said, as I took it from my pocket and showed it to her, and then slowly read it out from beginning to end.

"'And you believe I wrote that?' was all she said.

"In a moment I had her in my arms again and begged her to forgive me; but she said she would not till this matter was cleared up. So I began and told her all about it; but just as I was describing how I went, immediately after my arrival in Venice, to look at the house of Signor Faccioli, she cried out, —

"'Why, I know who's played you this cruel trick — it was Matteo Dà Ru!'

"'What on earth makes you think so?' I asked, already half convinced.

"'Well, he must have arrived from Spezzia by an earlier train than you did, for this morning he came to see my grandfather and immediately afterwards implored me to give him my troth, swearing that he had loved me for five years past. He begged for my love so passionately that I was a little frightened; so I put on an appearance of anger, and said scornfully that I would never wed him, even if I were free and he were not the son of Alessandro Dà Ru. Seeing I was in earnest, he suddenly drew himself up and left the room; but as he did so, I caught a glimpse of his pale face almost smiling, and I heard him muttering, 'Well, I've had my revenge.'

"*Ecco*, Signori! there's my story. I need n't tell you much more.

"We soon made all up between us again, and in less than a month Zena la Bionda and myself were married. Old Salvatore dowered her handsomely, and now, with the profits of my own gondola in addition, we are able to have all we want.

"Eh! what? you want to know what about that letter, and what about Matteo? Well, we took the letter that had caused so much trouble and sorrow to old Antonio Baruccio, the public scribe. He emphatically denied that it was in his handwriting, and he suddenly convinced us by showing beyond doubt (what I never thought of comparing) that the writing on the envelope and in the letter were decidedly different. We made him a confidant in the affair, and it was he who probably found the true solution when he declared that Matteo must have had the letter ready beforehand, and managed to exchange it for the true one when I handed him the letter to read. 'It was a very different note that I wrote last from the signorina's dictation,' added old Baruccio, with a sly laugh. Thereafter I sent Matteo a note to his father's house at Chioggia, and in that note I told him I had found out his treachery, and that he had better keep out of my way for some time to come. I added that I had kept the forged letter, and intended handing it over to the police. I got no answer to this note; but a few days later I heard that he had joined 'La Bella Bianca,' a merchant-ship trading between Livorno and San Francisco, and that he intended to settle down either in the latter place or in

Melbourne, where, amongst the small Italian colony, he had a well-to-do cousin. Anyway, he disappeared from this neighbourhood, and we have heard or seen nothing of him since.

"We are very happy, Signori, and if our little baby-girl (whom we named Gioja, because of the joy she brought us) grows up to be as fair a woman as her mother, I hope when her time comes that no 'Matteo' will come between her and her lover, to make their waiting perilous and hard to bear."

Thus Luigi finished his Venetian Idyl. We waited an hour or two longer under the cool and shadowy acacias of San Nicoletto; and then within about half an hour of sunset we left the Lido and sailed homeward past the desolate Jewish cemetery, where the dishonoured gravestones lie broken and half sunk amongst the nettles and scarlet poppies that grow upon the barren sand. As the prow of the gondola pointed straight between the Isola di San Giorgio and the Punta Motta, we saw Venice as she is not often seen, except in the sultry heats of late July or August. To the west, between Fusina and Mestre, the sky was of a black-purple, with a long broad band of orange-gold running through it. Nearer, overhead, flakes and curdled drifts of fiery crimson clouds spread out their fringed edges like red sea-weed torn and serrated by a furious tide; and over and beyond Venice itself great masses of cloud, tinged with lurid purplish russet and vivid bronze, slowly mounted upward and intermingled. Erelong we lost sight of this stormy splendour, for only a small portion of the sky was visible before us as we shot past the noble pile of the Salute.

We had hardly drawn up at our Traghetto, before a vivid flash of lightning darted in a long level line right from San Stefano past La Fenice, followed immediately by a wild crash of thunder. How the rain came down thereafter! It was as though a flood were whirling earthwards in deluging spray. Sitting comfortably drinking our coffee, we felt glad that our friend Luigi had a cosy home to take shelter in, and, to tell the truth, we rather envied him the greeting he was sure to get from Zena la Bionda and the crowing welcome of the little Gioja.

THE GRAVEN IMAGE.

The Graven Image.

Being the Narrative of James Trenairy.

THERE is an old house in Kensington which is to me, dweller in the remotest part of Cornwall though I am, the most solitary place I know. It is not far from the eastern boundary of Holland Park, yet, I am sure, few even of the residents on Campden Hill, or other Kensingtonians, are aware of its existence.

The house is a small square building, set far back in a walled garden. The approach is by an unattractive byway, which has all the appearance of a *cul-de-sac*, though there is really a narrow outlet which leads ultimately to High Street.

"The Mulberries," as it is called, was, some years ago, occupied by my father's old friend, John Tregarthen: as it was, in years back, by at least three successive John Tregarthens before him. The Tregarthens have always been a solitary and even somewhat eccentric race, but where the last representative of the family differed from his kin was in his dislike to his native Cornwall. He was the most confirmed Londoner I have ever known, though by this I mean only that he never left the metropolis, and seldom roamed beyond Kensington. So far as social intercourse was concerned, however, he might as well have lived in the light-house of Tre Pol, or at his own desolate ancestral home, Garvel Manor.

In the autumn of last year, on my way to spend the winter in Italy, I stayed for a few days in London. One afternoon I was in the Campden Hill neighbourhood, vainly in search of the studio of an artist friend, who seemed to me to have done his utmost to make his abode indiscoverable. It was while on this quest that I meandered through small streets and byways, and found myself at last at an unkempt gateway, whereon I could just decipher the words, "The Mulberries."

I confess that I had forgotten the very existence of Mr. John Tregarthen. Several years had passed since my father's death, and I had never had occasion to communicate with the owner of "The Mulberries." Now, however, that I was there, I was prompted by various feelings, but particularly by that clannish sentiment which distinguishes the true Cornishman, to seek Mr. Tregarthen himself.

To avoid needless details, I may say at once, and succinctly, that I found Mr. Tregarthen within; that he gave me a cordial welcome,—cordial, that is, for a man of so austere a life and so sombre a cast of mind; and that I was persuaded to remove my impedimenta from my Bloomsbury hotel, and to spend my two remaining spare nights at "The Mulberries."

When, a few hours later, I drove up to the house and rang the gate-bell, I feared that my host had forgotten our appointment and gone off on some errand or walk. Time after time I rang, but without any result; and as a dull November rain was drip-dripping from the few discoloured leaves still clinging to the chestnuts and elms, my position was not an agreeable one.

At last, however, Mr. Tregarthen came slowly along the garden path and opened the door to me. In the misty gloom, unrelieved by even a flickering gas-jet, I could not discern his features; but I fancied that he spoke constrainedly, and, indeed, as if he had already repented of his pressing invitation.

True, when once we were housed from the rain and chill, and the outer world was, as it were, locked away for the night, he became more genial, and even expressed heartily his pleasure at seeing me there as his guest. None the less, so gloomy was the lonely, silent house, so cheerless the aspect of the room where we sat, notwithstanding the bright flame of a wood fire and the yellow glow of a large reading-lamp, that I could not but regret the cheerful, if commonplace comforts of my hotel, the opulence of light and sound, the pleasant intimacy of familiar things enjoyed in common.

Still, I enjoyed my evening. We had a very simple dinner, for Mr. Tregarthen's one servant, an elderly Cornishwoman, was no vagrant from the culinary straight path to which she had been accustomed in her youth; but the wine was exceptionally good. My host talked well and intelligently, and, recluse though he was, I could see that he took at least a casual interest in the various matters of international policy which were at that time occupying so much attention in the press.

After dinner we adjourned to a small room, which he told me was his sanctum. There we had coffee, and sat for a long time in silence, watching the play of the firelight along the dark bookcases which lined the room, and listening to the dreary intermittent cry of the autumnal wind. Mr. Tregarthen had either forgotten, or had intentionally omitted, the lighting of his lamp. Though in ordinary circumstances, nothing delights me more than to sit and dream by the fireside in a dark room, I admit that on this occasion I should have preferred the serene company of a lamp, or even the unwavering effrontery of a gas jet. Again, I am a smoker, though indifferent to the pipe, and I could not but yearn for that postprandial luxury to which I had grown so accustomed. No cigar was offered, however, and I was quick to discover proofs that tobacco in any form was not to be found at "The Mulberries."

After a long silence, following some casual chit-chat about the places in Italy where I hoped to sojourn, my host suddenly made a remark that surprised me, wholly inconsequent as it seemed.

"You never knew him, did you?"

Again I noticed that strange constraint of voice, as if the mouth spoke while the mind was otherwise preoccupied.

"Him . . . whom?"

"My brother Richard."

"No, never. I heard —"

"What have you heard?" broke in Mr. Tregarthen, at once so imperiously and so sharply, and with so keen an accompanying glance the while he stooped in order to scrutinise me more fully in the upswing of the flame, that I realised his constraint was due to no mere dreamy indolence of mind.

"Oh, merely that he was always a wanderer, and that he came here at last broken in health, and died of some long-standing but mysterious trouble."

"Ah!" ejaculated my companion, and said no more. I did not care to broach the subject again, for I knew that it was one which could not be welcome. Indeed, I had heard more than I was willing to admit to Mr. Tregarthen, though I knew not how much was mere rumour. I remembered, however, that my father, a man as exact in the spirit of his statements as precise in the expression of them, had told me of some tragic misunderstanding having long separated John and Richard Tregarthen, and that there was something very strange in the return of the younger to his brother's house, whence he had departed years before with a curse upon him heavy as woe and unforgettable as death. Moreover, I recollected some vague particulars concerning a beautiful girl, one Catherine Tregaskis, belonging to an old family neighbouring our own, whom, as I understood, both men had loved, and who, in the manner of women, was a cause of infinite disturbance to both.

I was about to rise at last, for a fret of impatience was on me. The dull sound of the wind had grown to a moaning sough, that, in my then mood, could be hearkened with equanimity only in affluence of light and comfort. I thought that if I went to the bookcase near the fire my host would suggest the lighting of the lamp; but before I stirred, he broke the silence once more.

"We have scarce spoken of our own parts

yet. I wish to know something about our neighbours of old. Tell me, who lives now at Malfont? Is James Tregaskis still alive and well?"

"Yes," I replied, "Mr. Tregaskis is still alive, though he lives in as recluse a fashion as you do. His wife died three years ago. Childless and wifeless, the old man is very lonely. He has never been himself since — since —"

Here I stopped, embarrassed; but Mr. Tregarthen quietly finished my sentence, —

"Since the death of his daughter Catherine, you were going to say?"

I bowed slightly in affirmation.

"Will you tell me the actual wording of the inscription on the memorial tablet which he has raised in the family burial-ground behind the little private chapel on Malfont Heath?"

"Well — to say the truth, I don't know — that is to say, I have forgotten," I muttered, confusedly, reluctant as I was to communicate anything on a subject fraught with so much that would be painful.

"Does it run thus?" went on Mr. Tregarthen, quietly, though with a suggestion of irony in his voice. "Does it run thus, for I am sure you can at least correct me if I am wrong? First, the date of the year; and then —

"'To the Memory

of

Edward Tregaskis, aged 29 : Slain in war.
Olivia Tregaskis, aged 26 : Drowned at sea.
Catherine Tregaskis, aged 25 : Not yet avenged.'

Tell me, am I right?"

I admitted that he was, and even ventured to add that in our neighbourhood people thought trouble had perverted James Tregaskis' judgment.

"And, of course," I went on, "when he lost his youngest and best-loved child, the third terrible bereavement in a single year, it is no wonder that he imagined vain things, and turned away from those who would have won him to a more generous, if not a more resigned, view."

Mr. Tregarthen looked at me curiously, and I fancied that for a moment a sarcastic smile hovered across his face.

He said no more, however. After a brief interval he rose abruptly, lighted the lamp, and drew my attention to some rare books on Etrurian remains which he thought would interest me, as I was on my way to Volterra and other dead cities and towns of the Etruscan region.

I am not accustomed to late hours, and I suppose that I showed the weariness I felt. At any rate, when my host asked me if I was inclined to go to my room, I assented gladly.

Yet, when I was alone, my sense of sleep was no longer a pleasant languor. The room was a long oak-panelled chamber, both in height and appearance quite unlike what one would expect from an outside view of "The Mulberries." The bed, an old-fashioned four poster with heavy hangings, stood with its back to the same wall in which was the door; beyond it, on the right, was a fireplace, in which one or two logs sullenly smouldered. For the rest, there was nothing but a few stiff chairs set along the dark panelled walls, and a great gaunt badly-carved escritoire and bookcase of bog-oak.

I do not like gloomy rooms, and so it was natural that I should again think with regret of my comfortable lodging at the hotel, where, for old associations' sake, I always put up when I

The Graven Image.

go to London. But I had the good sense to undress and go to bed, hopeful of sleep.

Whether it was the singular silence within, or the moaning voice of the wind without, with a swift slash of rain ever and again upon the panes, or the coffee I had drunk, or I know not what, but sleep I could not. The longer I lay the more restless I became, and at last I thought I would rise and see if there were any readable volumes in the oak bookcase.

There were not, and I turned discontentedly to the fire, which I had replenished before I went to bed. I leaned on the mantelpiece for some time, looking into the flickering tongues and jets of red and yellow flame beneath, when I chanced at last to stand back and look up.

For the first time I noticed that what seemed a large bronze bas-relief was deeply set in the wall. I know not why I had not noticed it before; doubtless because the fire was low and the shadow deep, while I had not moved the candle away from the small book-table near the door where I had placed it on entrance.

I was glad of anything to distract me. So I lit my candle, and held it so that I could scrutinise the ornament, as it appeared to be. I saw at once that it was something out of the common. It seemed to be a sheet of bronze or copper, along the sides and at the base and summit of which were strange and perplexing arabesques and other designs, most notably what I presumed to be flaming swords, somewhat as represented by Leonardo da Vinci.

But in the centre was a head, life-size, which so far as I could tell was moulded in wax, hardened and tinted.

I did not apprehend these and other details till later, for my first feeling was one of startled curiosity, my second of something akin to fear.

The face was that of a woman; no doubt, of a beautiful woman, though the expression was so evil, or, rather, I should say, so forbidding, that I was blind to the native loveliness of the features.

What amazed me was the extraordinary lifelikeness. The face before me seemed almost as though it were alive. The clustering black hair, drawn back from the high pale brows, appeared to droop with its own weight; the compressed mouth, the distended nostrils, the intent staring gaze, simulated a painful and distressing actuality.

For some time I was fascinated by this strange portrait or imaginative study. I regarded it with something of the same blended curiosity and repugnance with which most of us look at some rare and terrible reptile. No, I felt sure, that woman *lived* once; through those sombre eyes came fire of passionate love or passionate hate; from those delicately-curved lips issued words fanged with scorn or sweet with perilous seduction.

At last I scrutinised the base. There, wrought in deep, strong lines, I read:

"THE GRAVEN IMAGE:"

with below it the words,

"*Lo, I made unto myself a graven image, that unto the end of my days the eyes of the body should likewise know no peace.*"

The inscription was mysterious, — nay, I admit that to me it had a terrifying suggestiveness.

I could look no more. Had I not been ashamed of my weakness, I should have dressed and gone down to the sitting-room. Determined, however, not to yield to my nervous disquiet, I went back to my bed. It was with a sense of relief that I felt my weariness growing upon me, and the stealthy tide of sleep draw nearer and nearer.

When I awoke, I know not how much later, it was with that abrupt sickening sensation which is indescribable, but is familiar to any one who has been aroused by the unheard but subtly apprehended entrance of another person into the room.

I lay for a few moments in a cold perspiration, trembling the while as though in terror. Then I opened my eyes.

I did not need to raise myself. The fire was burning dimly, but I could clearly see a woman standing beside it, looking fixedly into its embers. So much of her face as was turned towards me was in deep shadow. She was tall, and of a fine grace of figure, and though simply dressed in a long gown of a soft gray material, I imagined her to be of good birth and breeding.

I know not how it was that for that brief while fear left me, and that I could lie and speculate thus quietly. I perceived, of course, that my visitor was not Mr. Tregarthen's old servant, but it occurred to me that she might be an inmate of the house. For all I knew to the contrary, Mr. Tregarthen might be married; and, if so, this might be his wife or daughter come to my room unknowing me to be there, or, mayhap, as a victim to somnambulism.

But when suddenly a flame spurted upward from the heart of the fire, almost simultaneously with the sound of an approaching step along the passage, and the woman turned her face towards the door, so that I saw it plainly, my heart seemed as though it would burst.

For with a sense of unutterable fear I recognised in a flash the beautiful but terrifying face of the "Graven Image."

Startling as was the discovery, I had no time for thought, even if I had not lain as though paralysed.

The vindictive fury and scorn that shone in her eyes affrighted me. If it was Mr. Tregarthen who had come along the passage and was now knocking slowly at the door, his reception promised to be a dramatic one.

Whether the door opened or not, I cannot say. All I know is that I saw the woman draw back, as a tall dark man, whose features were quite unknown to me, slowly advanced.

Neither seemed to be aware of my presence; certainly they took no note of it.

I wondered he did not quail under that fierce, that inexpressibly malignant scorn.

As it was, he stopped abruptly. What tragedy of love turned to hate was this! In the dark scowl of the man I interpreted an insatiable fury. Yet I shuddered less at this speechless anger than at the lacerating contempt of her unwavering stare.

I looked to see the man spring at her, to do her some violence. But, leaning against the fireplace, he stood watching her intently. On her face was such a shadow of tempest as made me sick with a new and poignant terror.

I saw his lips move; the scowl on his face deepened. He drew himself erect, and as he did so I thought I heard him utter a name mockingly.

She did not answer, did not move. Outside I heard the wind rise and fall, monotonously crying in a thin shrewd wail. The patter of the rain had ceased, but so intense was the stillness that the drip, drip, from the soaked leaves upon the sodden ground was painfully audible.

Then so swiftly that I scarce saw her move, she sprang forward. There was a flash, a hoarse cry, and the man staggered back, with the blood from a knife-thrust spurting from his left shoulder.

She stood motionless. He, staring at her, panted hard as he slowly stanched the blood.

Suddenly she began to scream. I thought my blood would freeze with horror at the awful sound; scream after scream of deadly terror, and yet neither she nor the man moved.

But, looking at him, I saw that murder flamed in his eyes. Before I could spring from the bed to interfere, he leaped upon her like a beast of prey. In a moment both were on the floor, and I could see that he was strangling her to the death.

With a savage exclamation I dashed to the spot, but tripped, and the next moment lay unconscious, for my forehead fell against a corner of the oaken bookcase.

When I woke, or came out of my stupor, I was still on the floor where I had fallen, though the sunlight streamed in at the window. There was no sign of the horrible tragedy that had been enacted before me. With a shudder I looked at the "Graven Image," and recognised, with a new and horrible distinctness, the appalling verisimilitude of the waxen face.

It was impossible to remain in the room. I dressed hurriedly, and made my way downstairs. The front door was open, and I passed into the garden. The fresh air, damp as it was, was cool and soothing to my throbbing nerves, and, before long, I had almost persuaded myself that I had been victim to nightmare.

Suddenly I caught sight of Mr. Tregarthen. He was sitting in his sanctum, and beckoned to me. From the appearance of the room, and, indeed, of himself, I guessed that he had been there all night.

"Well?" he said, quietly: his sole greeting.

I thought it best to be frank.

"I have had a bad night," I began.

"I know it. I heard you cry out."

I looked at him amazedly and in some fear. Abruptly, I demanded, in an imperative tone:

"Who was the original of the 'Graven Image'?"

"Catherine Tregaskis, my betrothed wife."

I was silent, intensely surprised as I was.

Mr. Tregarthen leaned forward and handed to me a vignette portrait.

It was that of a handsome, dark-haired, dark-eyed, black-bearded man. I recognised the face at once, with a thrill of horrified remembrance.

"Who — who — is this man, Mr. Tregarthen?"

"My dead brother, Richard."

· · · · · · · ·

I write this a year after my visit to "The Mulberries," which I left that morning. Mr. Tregarthen is dead. "The Mulberries," under another name, is still untenanted; but I should be poor and forlorn indeed before I accepted again the shelter of that roof.

THE LADY IN HOSEA.

The Lady in Hosea.

I.

"And she shall follow after her lover, but she shall not overtake him; and she shall seek him, but shall not find him; then shall she say, I will go and return to my first husband; for then was it better with me than now!—"
HOSEA.

WHEN John Dorian, with the help of the poker and the flaming coals, had demolished Dream No. LIII. and last, he lit a cigar. Then he lay back in a deep, padded armchair, in order to enjoy to the full his evening paper.

The effort had been exhausting. He was a sentimentalist, and had been wont to mark his love-letters, after they had reached the tenth, as "Dream I.," "Dream II.," and so on. True, he had not gone through the whole fifty-three that night. The little india-rubber bands which had been round Claire's letters lay beside the ash-tray on the mantelpiece, like an angler's heap of worms, discarded because of their premature death; but the pile could not have consisted of more than about a score and a half. As a matter of fact, Dreams XV. to XXI. had escaped the ruthless poker. Covered with kisses, warmed with sighs, they had been cremated in the late days of June. They were — I should say had been — animated by aspirations of soul-union, assurances concerning Immortality, and perfectly lucid and frank expositions of a vivid passion. In a word, they were so explicit that John Dorian had found himself forced to submit them to a double committal: first, to his heart (as he designated his memory), and then to the fire. Again, Dreams XLV. to LI. had, though autumnal, endured a like fate. True, they were without any remarks about Immortality; on the other hand, the union of mind, soul, and body, particularly the third partner in the trinity, was emphasised in them with ardour, eloquence, and a pleading yearning.

By an accident, five missives from another lady had been tied up with those from Claire.

These had been discovered one Sunday, when, unwell with a chill, and brooding upon the immortality of a great passion, Dorian had permitted himself the dangerous luxury of a reperusal of his love-letters. Only skilled *chefs* should attempt pleasant surprises in the way of *réchauffés*.

In the peaceful quiet of that Sabbath afternoon thirteen epistles had been done to death: seven, too passionate, from Claire; five, too financially exigent, from Mademoiselle Phalène.

Thus it was that on this October night John Dorian, on demolishing the discarded raiment of his Dreams, confided to the appreciative secrecy of his fire no more than four-and-thirty burning missives. The epithet is hyperbolical; but there is no doubt about its actuality in the past participle.

A few weeks ago " Dream LIII." would have meant to him no more than the fifty-third kiss he had received from Claire. It would have been simply a delightful link between Fifty-two and Fifty-four. But when LIII. is endorsed " and last," the number stands forth from its fellow-figures, the elect of Fate.

An effort? Yes; it had been an effort to

read through, latterly to glance at, those thirty-four remnants of an undying passion.

Dorian had two small ivory figures by the sculptor Dampt. They ornamented his twin bookcases by the fire-side; above the shelves to the right, "Aspiration," with upraised arms and trance-wrought face; above the shelves to the left, "Consummation," supine, satisfied, with wearied eyes.

He looked at the little group to the left, while Dream LIII. emitted the unpleasant odour of waste paper aflame. He smiled unwittingly; then, wittingly, sighed. Then he lit his cigar, seated himself, and leisurely unfolded the news-sheet.

The "leader" interested him. Halfway down the column on the ensuing page, "The Casket of Pandora," he read: "The Lover is ever a sophisticator."

"True," he muttered indolently, while he stretched his feet nearer the fire-glow; "how true! one sophisticates oneself with dreams of impossible virtues and charms."

"Sophisticator!" he resumed. "Let me see what the dictionary has to say, if there *is* such a word."

With a slight effort, he obtained the volume he sought from the swing-bookcase near his chair.

"Ah! here we are: *sophistical, sophisticate, sophisticator*. H'm. . . . '*Sophisticator*:' 'one who adulterates, debases, or injures the purity of anything.'"

The dictionary must have become limp from long disuse, for in a few seconds it slipped to the floor, and lay there, unheeded, in a dead faint.

A hunted look had come into John Dorian's eyes, but it passed. For some time he stared blankly into the fire. Then, suddenly, he resumed his perusal of the "Quadrant Gazette."

With a yawn, he skipped the "Casket of Pandora" column. "These paragraphists," he muttered, "either talk rubbish, or bore one with their rehashed hash."

There was wind without. It came down the street, at times, blowing a loud clarion: a minute later it would swirl away again, with a rattling fanfaronade among the chimney-tops. Now and again a flurry of rain slapped the window-panes.

It was certainly comfortable by the fire.

Possibly it was sheer tampering with luxury that made Dorian rise and wander restlessly about the room.

The rumble of the Piccadilly omnibuses outside emphasised the cheerful quietude of the room.

Its solitary occupant wavered between a cabinet in one corner filled with blue china, and, in another corner, an escritoire. This lured him. He seated himself in front of it, opened a drawer, and, taking out and unfolding a diary, glanced at page after page. An entry in August arrested his attention.

"*August* 21.—Still here at Llandynys. Did not leave on Monday, as Cecil T. was summoned to Chester on some magisterial matter. He expected to be back that night, but wired that he would be detained two or three days, and hoped I would prolong my stay. I did. Claire brought me the message. Her eyes were lovely. She knew I would stop. What days these have been! Never, never shall I forget them! What a deep joy it is that she and I are so absolutely one with the other! To think of it; she Claire; I, John Dorian, at one forever and ever! There can be no end to a passion such as ours. It is the nobler, the stronger, because of our great renunciation. Neither she nor I will leave Cecil Trevor a mourner. Indeed, it would be cruel if, having by undreamed-of hazard taken royal possession of his wife's heart, I should also break up his home by removing her to another clime as *my* wife. No, we will be strong. Love has been compassionate, and given each unto each. What need to go to the last extremity — a bitter one at the best. No; there will be no elopement. But I am hers and she is mine, in life and death. Ah, *Death!* No! no! no death for us! For all eternity our love shall endure. She and I, I and she, together forever and ever."

Dorian closed the diary with a snap. Rising, he replaced the book, and then walked slowly to the window. He drew back the blind. The cloud-rack was broken for an interval; overhead, like dark, frozen water between ice-banks, he could see a width of sky. A planet, a score or more of stars, glistered icily.

"For all eternity," he muttered; "I and she, she and I, forever and ever." For a few minutes he was silent, motionless, profoundly intent. Then he smiled.

"Ah, I was always a star-gazer!"

With that he went back to his chair in front of the fire, took up a new magazine in lieu of the newspaper, and made ready to enjoy himself.

Doubtless he would have succeeded, but fate willed otherwise. The tap of a postman was the particular disguise taken by Nemesis.

"A letter for you, sir," said his man, holding out a salver on which was a business-looking envelope.

"H'm. Just wait a moment, George. Ah!—ah! it's from Anderson & Anderson. . . . George, are you there?"

"Yes, sir."

"George, if a lady should call for me to-night or to-morrow, you are to tell her I am not here. Say—oh! let me see—say that she is just too late; that I left this morning for Paris, *en route* for the East. Tell her I won't be back again for years."

"If she wants me to take or send you any message?"

"In that case tell her that you will certainly do so; only, add that it had better not be urgent, as you don't expect to join me in the East till after I telegraph to you from—let us say Egypt."

"Very good, sir."

The man hesitated, fidgeted, but thought better of his intent, whatever it was. As soon as he had gone Dorian eagerly scanned the note he had received. It was from a firm of solicitors, and was to the effect that it was true Mrs. Cecil Trevor had left her home, that she had called to ask his, John Dorian's, address, and that to-morrow if not to-day, or the day after if not to-morrow, she would certainly obtain it from someone.

It is a common mistake to say that Nemesis never blunders. That policeman of the gods can, and does, sometimes appear on the scene too soon, or too late, or otherwise inopportunely. He came down Piccadilly a second time this evening, disguised this time as Claire Trevor.

Dorian was halfway through his second cigar when he heard a hansom stop beneath his windows. This was followed by a tap at the front-door. To the tap succeeded the opening of the door; then a sustained conversation.

"I am no coward," said John Dorian, "but I will retire — ah! — to the bath-room!"

II.

Mrs. Trevor, as she sat before the fire in her room in the Whitehall Hotel, did not know whether to laugh or cry. This was not because she was either amused or chagrined, but because she believed her heart was broken. There are women, as there are men, who, fronting irredeemable disaster, with a heart almost callous on account of its pain, scarce know whether laughter or sobs shall best ease them.

Claire Trevor had taken the step which experience tells should never be taken: that is, she had burnt the ship of her married life. All manner of misadventure may be wrought against that vessel, but it should never be burnt; at least not until another has been boarded by invitation, and a license as first mate duly obtained. In other words, she had not only left her home and husband, but had also been rash enough to leave a letter behind her for Cecil Trevor. It told him that she loved, and was loved by, John Dorian; that she could not live without the said John, and that it would be criminal on her part to remain a day longer with him, Cecil, as his wife. Lest there should be any mistake, she had added a few particulars.

She had no children. She did not love Cecil Trevor: but she had not suspected this until — well! The suspicion developed into a fact when, after a few months' acquaintanceship, John Dorian read her his two-act play, "For Better, for Worse." At the moving sentimentality which did duty as a dramatic close, he had informed her that she was the heroine, Helen, and he Paris, the hero.

In the process she lost a few ideals. These are seldom missed at first, and it was some time before she realised that they were gone. She sighed, with true feeling, but said to herself that she would be brave.

One ideal, however, she did hold, not only dear and intimate, but inviolate. This was the chivalrous love, the unalterable devotion, of John Dorian.

It had not been without difficulty that she obtained his new address. Circumstances had kept them apart for three months, and in that time he had shifted his quarters more than once.

For a woman without much intuition, it is to her credit that she was not only undeceived by the instructed lie of Dorian's valet, but at once guessed that her lover wished "Finis" to be written to their romance. She had little imagination, and she did not understand how this finality could be; but she felt it in the very core of her heart. The tragi-comedy had fizzled out while, having left without an attempt to expostulate with, or even to force an interview upon, her lover, she drove back to her hotel.

For a long time she had stared into the fire, till her eyes ached. At last she rose, and took two photographs from her leather-covered desk. The insolent light of the gas flamed upon her. By a vague instinct she turned it lower, and also avoided a glimpse of herself in the adjacent mirror.

There was ample light to see the photographs by. One was of a man about five-and-thirty, tall, elegant, graceful even, evidently dark, with oval dusky eyes, short hair with a wave in it at the sides, clean contours, a sensitive nose and mouth, a self-conscious smile on the face, the hands artistic, but with the thumbs noticeably lifted backward. A good-looking man of the world, in most judgments, no doubt. To a close and keen observer everything, from the thumbs to the pointed ears, betokened the refined and cultured animal which had the arrogance to believe it was kin to Apollo, and the blindness not to see that it was of the brotherhood of Pan the Satyr. All the possibilities of the epileptic slept in that comely exterior. The life in him was a phosphorescent fungus in a grave.

Mrs. Trevor took the ordinary view. The photograph pained her by its tantalising truth. Long and earnestly as she looked at it, she stared longer and more intently at the other. It represented a young woman who could not have passed her twenty-seventh year; blonde, with a graceful figure. That, really, was all you or I might discern were we to come upon the likeness in an album. Claire Trevor, however, saw more. She evoked a woman whose tender heart gave a lovely life to the blue eyes, an exquisite, unwhispered whisper to the lips. She saw the rippling fair hair moving in the warm breath of her lover. Within, she beheld a strong and heroic mind fronting the Shadow of Fate — an undaunted, unselfish, greatly daring Soul. As a matter of fact, what she saw were some rainbow-shimmerings from a land where she had never fared. A great number of other people's thoughts occupied almost every available cell in her brain, and the accommodation for her own mind was almost as limited as that dusty back-parlour wherein her soul (without a capital) lay bedridden and blind.

The past tense should have been more emphasised. Probably that evening a few more cells had been opened, and others summarily usurped by tyrannical new-comers. As for the invalid in the back-parlour, it had doubtless risen, and was fumbling about in the dark.

When Mrs. Trevor seated herself again she took Dorian's photograph and laid it between two coals which glowed vehemently, despite the corroding ash at their base. The card crackled, shrivelled, and became a malodorous nonentity. A minute or two elapsed before Claire's photograph was likewise cremated. It fell sideways, and in the spurt of redeeming flame she read the date of the night when she had given herself to John Dorian,—a night which had succeeded an evening of singular beauty, wherein the stars moved with a polar magnificence of light, and yielded in glory only to the promise of eternity which the uncontrolled passion of two hearts discerned in the frosty indifference of those remote luminaries.

Even a cremated passion does not add fuel to a fire. Perhaps the fire resents the intrusion of a quenched flame, particularly if it, too, has been slowly dying. At any rate, the photographs of two aspirants for immortality ended in smoke. To expedite the burial Mrs. Trevor stooped, to utilise the poker. As she reached forward, a locket swung from her bosom, struck the mantelpiece, and hung open, its two sides outspread, as though it were a metallic butterfly, the emblem of hope.

She relinquished her intention, though as a matter of fact the service of the poker was not now needed.

Instead, she sat back, and stared at the miniature in the locket. It was an excellent likeness of Cecil Trevor. Looking at it, she could see every feature of her husband: his rather furrowed brow, fairly well marked; his heavy eyebrows and calm hazel eyes; his heavy, straight nose, with its rigid nostrils; his slightly curly brown beard, unbroken from the ear-level, and in the vogue of Henry VIII.; his large, ill-formed, but kindly mouth; his coarse jowl and dogged chin. She knew that he was taller than the broad squire suggested in the miniature, and also that his voice was softer than a stranger would infer. And as she looked she believed she saw something in the eyes she had never seen before.

With a cry she rose, then sank to her knees, and hid her face in her hands, while her hair swept the chair like a creeper over a ruin.

The fire had almost subsided into ash when she rose and slowly began to undress. She pondered the advisability of a prayer, but, on second thoughts, decided not to intrude herself just then on an offended and probably resentful Providence. There would be ample time on the morrow, when she would feel more purged of her sin.

"I will go back," she whispered to herself. She lay down in the vague discomfort of a new loneliness. "I will go back. Perhaps he will forgive; perhaps he will let me atone; perhaps he loves me still."

The invalid inmate of the back-parlor murmured indistinctly, "Oh, what a fool, *what* a fool you have been!"

III.

When Claire Trevor reached the station for Llandynys, it was to learn that she was a widow.

During the long drive she wept sincerely for her resurrected affection, now so untimely slain.

Did Cecil now know all? Do the dead see, understand? The thought troubled her; but she did not disguise from herself that she was more anxious as to how much he knew when he was alive.

"Death, the result of an accident in the hunting-field." That was what she had been told. The accident had occurred in the afternoon of the morning when she had taken her fatal step. There was just a chance Mr. Trevor had not seen the insensate letter she had written.

That drive aged Mrs. Trevor. She felt as though she were driving away from her youth.

At the threshold of her home — if it still was her home — she was met by the Vicar. His manner was deeply sympathetic and considerate, — so considerate that she inferred safety so far. The Vicar's profound respect indicated her acceptance in his eyes as the heiress of Llandynys.

Claire Trevor never quite forgave herself, because when she looked upon the corpse of her husband, she saw only, thought of only, dreaded only, the letter he held in his folded hands.

"What does it mean?" she whispered hoarsely to Mr. Barnby.

"Your last letter," the Vicar replied with tender unction. "It was brought to him before the end by the servant, who had forgotten to deliver it before his master went out riding. He was too weak to open it. He kissed it just before he died. When he pressed it against his heart, the heart had already stopped. Take it, my dear madam, take it; it will be a lovely memento for you for the rest of your life."

FRÖKEN BERGLIOT.

Fröken Bergliot.

In the summer heats few foreigners are to be seen at Castel Gandolfo. Half-a-dozen Roman families may be settled in villas round the hill-set Lake of Albano; and a stray artist, a Spaniard or Southern Frenchman most likely, may lodge for a few days in the little town. In August, however, most people who can afford to leave Rome at all go to the sea or to the mountains. For, though Castel Gandolfo is as high and breezy a place as any in the Alban hills except Rocca di Papa and perhaps Nemi, the heat there can be oppressive, and the dreaded malaria sometimes steals up from the Campagna, though not till after it has visited Genzano and l'Ariccia and even Albano itself.

Nemi is lovelier, but there is no more picturesque spot in the Alban range than Castel

Gandolfo, that ancient summer-home of so many Popes, and beloved of Romans since the days of the Cæsars. On its lofty crest, amid its pines and ilexes and cypresses, it looks down on the one side upon the beautiful Lake of Albano, a vast amethyst as it seems in summertide, and upon the steep volcanic slopes of Alba reaching upward in a splendid semicircle. From the other, it looks across the Campagna, upon desolate leagues of pale blue in the morning, upon a shimmering haze of mist at noon, and again upon leagues upon leagues of purple at wane of day. Behind the high-set village run the two lovely ilex-avenues to Albano; beyond it, or rather beyond the Papal palace and gardens that give the little town its name, goes straight as an arrow for a while the high road to Rome.

It is a place wherein to eat the lotos, to dream dreams. In the morning, when the sky is of a lustrous blue and when the hill-air blows freshly down the slopes from Rocca di Papa, one can rest for hours looking upon the ruffled lake, watching the fish leap, listening to the wind among the ilexes or the chestnuts. In the late afternoon the watcher upon the lower western wall will see the most impressive sight in the world, — the sun passing in a purple veil of mystery athwart the desolate expanse of the Campagna, shedding an evanescent flame of light upon the dark patch in the distance that is Rome, and illumining as with green or crimson fire the remote marge of the Tyrrhenian Sea.

Three years ago the mid-Italian summer was exceptionally hot. Drought prevailed, and on many of the upland pastures the grass was in colour like newly-tanned leather. On the Campagna cattle sickened, and human beings died or crawled to and fro stricken with the ague of malaria. The hill-towns of the Alban and Volscian mountains were full of ragged, wild-eyed shepherd-folk; even of sea-dwellers from the pestilential shores of *Etruria Maritima*, the desolate tract from the base of the mountains of Volterra to the Pontine Marshes near the frontier of the old kingdom of Naples.

All through those torrid weeks of July and August, Bergliot Rossi was as one in a restless trance. It was the third year since this girl out of the north had come to live with her uncle, Ernesto Rossi, the antiquary. She now hated this glaring, burning south that had appealed to her so much at first; hated this stifling heat, this inland weariness, this malaria that everywhere brooded as an invisible beast of prey; hated even the Alban hill-folk, with their hard voices, their inhospitable ways, their witless turning of the dear Scandinavian "Bergliot Ross" into "Bergliota Rossi," as of her aunt's name "Hedwig" into "Eviga."

How gladly, she often murmured — and thought ever — would she have stayed in her beloved Norway when her father, Captain Henrik Ross, went to join the wife whom he had lost twenty years before. She would have known poverty, and perhaps, at first, chagrin, — for Henrik Ross had lived well, and with even better pretensions than his means warranted; but she would have been among her own nation, with the sweet Norsk voice and tongue to charm her ears, and within sight of the mountains, within sight of the sea. To be away from Norway seemed to her a fate to sympathise with; to be away in the far south, with a northern soul, and to see no more the dark mountains and the wild, beautiful, changeful Scandinavian seas, was to be indeed worthy of sorrowful pity.

Still, Uncle Ernest and Aunt Hedwig had been kind, and to be in that lovely hill-village, and so near the mysterious city in whose name is the supreme metropolitan sound, was a subdued joy. But long before Aunt Hedwig's death, at the end of the second year of Bergliot's exile, the girl had wearied of the south, and was consumed by an abiding passion for the lost north. This passion haunted her dreams by night, and lent to her diurnal visions what was akin to anguish. The winter she could endure, particularly if the ice lay on the pools and rivulets, and when the snow covered the woodland ways all over the hill-tract from Frascati to Velletri. The spring was so beautiful that, though she longed for the leagues of gorse and the green fiords of "home," she could not but rejoice in the exceeding loveliness. Fröken Bergliot, as she wished always to be called, became a well-known wanderer among the towns and villages. In l'Ariccia and Genzano the women thought the Norse signorina a little "touched"; for the rest, they despised what they could not understand. Latterly, she avoided these places, preferring to wander through the upland coppices to Nemi; or to climb to high Rocca di Papa, where the children are seized sometimes by vertigo and are killed before their mothers can snatch them from the sheer slopes; or even to make her way through the woodlands above Frascati to the old ruins of Tusculum. But best she loved to linger in the ilex-avenue overlooking the Campagna, when afternoon merged into twilight, and no sound broke the stillness save distant bells summoning to *Ave Maria*, and, above in Castel Gandolfo, the cries and laughter of children; or, through the hot noontide, to lie on the steep incline to the south of the old Papal palace, and look down upon the lake, and dream of green fiords and precipitous rocks, yellow-gray with sea-moss and lichen, furrowed by ocean rains and the salt sea-wind. When the summer heats set in, however, her nostalgia for the beloved north became an abiding pain. She panted in the hot breath of air and earth as might a caged swift in a room. She felt as though she would die if she were to stay much longer in this foreign land, among this alien folk. An immense loneliness possessed her. It was as though she were a castaway. Her Uncle Ernest was a taciturn man, much absorbed in his vocation and its connected studies, and was, moreover, often away for days at a time, in Rome, or Florence, or Naples, or even farther afield. In these solitary hours she would go wearily to and fro, conscious of little save her overmastering desire to see the north once more; to feel its cool breath in her mind and in her spirit as well as upon her body; to hear the lap-lapping of the waves; to watch the white sea-horses leap in the sunlight when, at the fiord-mouth, a mountain-wind tore against the tide-race. If, in these moments of intense longing, she descried, trailed across the sky like a thin Japanese eyebrow, a flight of northward-winging birds, she would turn away sobbing in her bitter pain, or throw herself upon the ground and seek relief in tears.

But, alas! she had not a *soldo* of her own in the world. Uncle Ernest gave her nothing. She had a home; she had food, clothes, even a few luxuries, or what in that remote life were looked upon as luxuries; she had the precious violin which she had bought from her uncle with the small sum that Aunt Hedwig had given her shortly before her death. But to reach even Florence — to gain the Alps — how could one do this? There was but one way: to fare afoot, to beg food and shelter. This she could not do, for she was bound in honor to her uncle. Sometimes she thought she would give lessons in violin-playing; but unfortunately she was herself in sore need of instruction, and none of the rich foreigners who lived some weeks or months near Albano or Frascati would employ an undisciplined amateur. Again, she even dreamed that she might gain work in teaching Italian to the children of Scandinavian visitors; but in the first place her Italian was not good, and in the next, and conclusively, no rich Scandinavians ever did come to the Alban slopes. Once, before the Signora Eviga was laid in the little cemetery beyond the pinewood, Bergliot had met the Norwegian consul in Rome, and he had promised to bear her wish in mind; but she had heard nought of him since then, and even feared, what was indeed the case, that her uncle had discouraged the idea.

And now in this hot August, the third she had known in Italy, she realised that all the savour had gone out of her life. She no longer cared whether she survived to fulfil her few household duties to Uncle Ernest, or was laid beside Aunt Hedwig, the silent old Norse lady who, while speaking in Italian to her Roman nurse, suddenly said in Norsk, "Jeg er troett," "I am tired," and was dead.

One morning after a sleepless night she rose ere daybreak. A fever of unrest was upon her. If only Uncle Ernest had not been ailing of late, she could no longer have withstood the temptation to take her violin and play her way back to the dear northland that called her from afar.

She did not know why she struck along by the goatherds' path that led by the eastern heights to the slopes between Frascati and Tusculum. She had not been at the last-named since January, and then the snow had lain thick in the hollows, and she had cried with delight when slipping often up the steep frozen lane that leads from Frascati. Perhaps some vague memory of the coolness and whiteness led her thither.

It was sunrise as she came to a glade a short distance below the bluff overhanging the ancient ruins. She stood for a time, with her outstretched left hand holding a sycamore branch, and her whole figure wrought to an alert motionlessness. A slight flush was upon her beautiful face, paler than its wont, owing to summer-languor and sleepless nights and the long strain of unsatisfied longing. In her eyes, gray-blue in general but now almost violet, was a flame of azure light. The sun-ray that was tangled in the wave of her brown hair twisted and turned in gold, and passing and coming again and again, left an amber shimmer in the sweet brown duskiness.

But though her joy was of the risen sun, of the new day that came in radiant beauty, — stirring afresh the Norland passion in her for sky and sea and the upland air and mountainous aspects, — she was intent also because of what she heard. A song filled the glade with music. The unseen singer was advancing, and his brave lilt leaped to her ear.

While she stood entranced, herself a vision

of morning music embodied, she saw the musician. He was a young man, tall, robust, as fair of skin and azure-eyed as herself, with close-clustered hair tawny as sunlit shallows in a brook.

The song ceased. The young man had seen the girl, an unexpected vision indeed, at that hour, in that place, in that country. She appeared to him as something ideal. Artist as he was, he had noted immediately and keenly the loveliness of her colour, the perfection of her form, the happy accident of her pose. "Ah! I have found my point of view now," he exclaimed; "*here* is my 'morning glory' picture ready for me!"

Bergliot slowly let her arm fall. The flicker of the sycamore leaves sent dusky shadows across her face. She hesitated, and then took a step forward.

The stranger was coming towards her. Her heart-beat quickened. This sweet singer, out of the golden morning, was a Norlander too; there could be no mistake about that, she thought with gladness. Was he a Norsk, a Swede, a Dane? Perhaps a German or an Englishman?

But at that moment she felt a touch upon her arm. Looking round, she saw Anita, the little daughter of Ermerilda Lanza, the woman whom her Uncle Ernest employed to do the cooking and rough work at his house.

"What is it, Anita?"

The child looked at her for a moment in amazement. The caressing voice was suddenly grown hard, the gentle eyes were of a cold starry radiance.

"I have run . . . run hard, signorina," she panted; "my mother sent me. The Signor Rossi is angry with you. He is about to go to Venezia, and he wants to see you before he goes. He asked thrice for you last evening, but you were not to be found, and when he asked again, late, you were in bed and asleep."

Bergliot turned and looked dreamily back upon the wooded slope, now aglow with sunlight. The young man had stopped, and was looking fixedly towards her.

"Who is *he* — is he a friend?" Anita asked, with childish curiosity.

"He . . . . he is the voice of the North," replied the girl, as if in a reverie. Then, turning again abruptly, and without another look upon what she was leaving, she set off at a rapid pace, with Anita trotting behind her, and was soon lost to view among the coppices.

Old Marco Gozzi, the charcoal-burner, on his way to Rocca di Papa from Frascati, nodded to her as she passed, and muttered that it made him young again to see that lovely image of his Caterina, a fair Venetian damsel who fifty years back had withered of the inland weariness and died, long before her vagrant muleteer of a husband had fallen into the drear estate of a charcoal-burner.

He was still looking after her, or rather upon the way by which she had gone, when he heard some one approach, and, turning, beheld the stranger. He recognised him as the painter who, three days before, had given him a five-lire piece for sitting for his portrait. No doubt the man was mad, Marco thought; but madmen with five-lire pieces for free disposal were persons to be treated with respect.

"Buon giorno, Signor Pittore!"

"Ah! buon giorno, buon giorno, Marco mio! So we are both up betimes! Well, it's the only way in this hot weather. I say, Marco, who was that signorina who passed you a little ago?"

"The signorina? Oh, well," stammered the man, with that strange evasive instinct so often shown among Italians in remote places, "it is of no importance. Eh, what, *per Bacco*, yes, I remember; she is called Anita, daughter of Ermerilda Lanza, of Castel Gandolfo."

"Not the wife of that scoundrel Michele Lanza . . . . that would be —"

"*Si, signore, si.*"

"But, man, that lovely girl could not be the daughter of a coarse brute like Michele Lanza. Why, he, and his Ermerilda too, if I remember rightly, are both as dark as a coal-pit, and this girl is like a northener."

"Ah, the signor pittore means the tall one?"

"Why, you silly idiot, whom do you think I meant? Come, Marco, don't be a fool. See here; tell me all you know, and you shall have a lira with which to drink my health."

"Why, *eccellenza*, every one about here knows who she is. All the young men are in love — and vainly in love — with the Signorina Bergliota. She is the niece of the Signor Antiquario Ernesto Rossi, a reputable man, though a foreigner, saving your worthy presence, signor pittore. Old Rossi lives in the end house at the top of the *via* in Castel Gandolfo leading to the lower Albano Road. He lives alone there, he and his niece. The woman Lanza helps her."

"Bergliota .... the name is not an Italian one. Why, of course, it's Bergliot. Are they Norsk?"

"God knows. 'T is very likely. They are Tedeschi; that's all I know."

"She lives alone with him, you say?"

"Yes; worse luck for her."

"Why?"

"Because of the old man's temper. He has a fiend of a temper, I assure you."

"Well, good day, Marco. The saints send you luck." And with a good-humoured smile and wave of his hand, Torquil Bärnson turned away. For some reason he did not wish to accompany Marco and listen to his chit-chat about the Signorina Bergliota. As he made his way up the slopes to Rocca di Papa, the music of a woman's name came and went upon his lips with ever fresh recurrence.

"*Fröken Bergliot—Fröken Bergliot—Fröken*

Bergliot," he muttered over and over; and often a sudden smile of delight, as when one comes upon a new flower or listens to the first lark-song of spring, came upon his face.

When he did reach Rocca di Papa he had lost all inclination for his work. The landscape he had begun seemed sunless, lifeless. He wanted to paint his long projected "Morning Glory." Down in the woods of the Papal villa he heard the thrushes call. The sweet repetitive note that gave the welling lilt to their song was *Bergliota — Bergliota.* From the steep crag just below the village, where he lay adream in the sunshine, he could hear the wavelets far below lap-lapping in the sedges, or with slow wash lisping under the overhanging alders and ashes that with the twisted olives fringed the lake-marge. And this sweet sound that rose like incense through the golden-yellow air was *Fröken Bergliot — Fröken, Fröken Bergliot.*

The afternoon was almost gone when the young Norse painter roused himself from his happy indolence. To his own surprise, perhaps, and certainly to that of the few heat-sleepy villagers who watched him, he walked vigorously along the steep mule-path that led along the old crater-edge till it joined the Marino Road to Castel Gandolfo. For in August no one did anything energetically. Even the few foreigners who lingered in the neighbourhood employed the afternoon in the luxury of the siesta. No one but a poor devil of a painter, said the peasants, would be about at that season. The innkeeper himself, at whose house in Marino Torquil Bärnson lodged, thought that his good-looking visitor must be very hard up that he had to rise at daybreak and go dabbing paint upon a canvas throughout the hot day. To Torquil himself, indeed, came more than once a shy recognition of the fact that his sudden energy was surprising. Only the day before he had admitted to himself that while winter, spring, and summer, in Rome and its neighbourhood, were delightful, the early autumn lacked both solace and joy for a northerner. "Oh, for a breath of the Blue Fiord!" he had cried again and again, filled with longing for his sea-swept home.

But when he came to the junction of the roads he did not turn towards Marino. He had remembered that he wanted advice on some matter which only an antiquary could determine for him. This point presented itself as in urgent need of solution. There was not a day to spare, though it had occurred to him more than a year ago. Besides, did he not owe a visit of courtesy to his fellow-countryman, Ernest Ross — the two of them probably at that time the only Norsemen within reach of the Alban hill-wind? Of course he did. And was not Herr Ross a man of distinction, to whom it was only civil to pay one's respects? Now that he thought of it, had he not heard him spoken of in Bergen as one of the most remarkable, — one of the most remarkable — oh, to be sure, one of the most remarkable archæologists — no, antiquarians — of the day?

Is it not Firdusi of Persia who says that a young man in love is more shy than a wild roe?

Visible shyness there was, indeed, when Torquil Bärnson knocked at the door of Signor Rossi's lodging in Castel Gandolfo.

There was no response. If any one within heard his repeated summons it was only to treat it with sublime indifference. At last a woman, leaning from a neighbouring window, suggested that it was useless to wake all Castel

Gandolfo, as Signor Ernesto Rossi had gone away.

"Will he be here to-morrow?" Torquil ventured, with undue eagerness.

"No. He has gone among foreigners. He is faring as far as Venice — the Blessed Mother knows where else. He will not be here for weeks. The old man swore he might never come again."

"Ah-h! And — and — the signorina?"

"Ha! ha! the signorina!"

"Well, what of her?" asked Torquil, sharply, alert in resentment, for the woman's voice was a sneer.

"Oh, *la bella Bergliota*, no fear for *her*. She will do well enough."

"Is she within?"

"No."

"Where is she?"

"Find out for yourself."

Torquil saw he had made a mistake. The ice in his voice had frozen this bubbling well of gossip. The woman, who looked at him angrily, was heavy and vulgar, but had once been pretty.

"Ah, you beautiful women are all alike," he

said lightly; "but if *la bella* Bergliota *has* gone, why, then Castel Gandolfo has still got *you*."

The ice was melted, wholly lost. The well o'erbrimmed.

"Ah, signore, how sad it is that the good Signor Ernesto should be so worried with his niece! True, he has gone far this time, very far. But who can blame him wholly?"

"What has he done this time?"

"Oh, when he wanted to see his niece this morning early, behold no Bergliota was to be found anywhere. When at last she did come — after Ermerilda's Anita had scoured the whole country for her — the old man was furious. He called her a useless slut. He vowed he wished she had never come to Castel Gandolfo."

"What did *she* say?"

"Oh, she up with her head like a wild goat o' the hills, and said that she was quite ready to go back to Norway. 'Go, then,' cried her uncle, 'and never let me see you again; for, truth to tell, I am tired of you — and further truth to tell, I am going to bring the widow Lucia Lucchesi from Rome to share bed and board with me, and the good wife won't care to have *you* idling about.' And with that he went to his cabinet, and taking from it a small purse, he put some gold in it and flung it at her, saying it was more than she was worth, but he gave it so that no one could say he turned his own kindred from his door without a *soldo* to bless herself with."

"And she?" And as Torquil spoke with eager heed, the woman noticed the flush on his face and the bright light in his eyes.

"She? She took it of course, and glad to get it. It's more than she —"

"Yes; but in what way did she take it — what did she say?" interrupted the young man, with a twinge of regret at learning that Bergliot had not returned a gift given with a churlishness so rude.

"Ha! ha! At first she grew as red as a peony. The flush went over her face like wine spilt in the lake — came and went just like that. I almost thought that she was going to refuse to take the money. The idea! She was acting — chit! But suddenly she turned again. 'The servant is worthy of her hire,' she said quietly; and with that she took the purse, put it in her pocket, and then, holding out her hand to Signor Rossi, said something in her own language which I guessed to be a request to shake hands in farewell. However, I know no more, save that Ernesto Rossi went away in Andrea Placci's wine-cart at eight o' the clock, and that before noon Bergliota packed her things, said good-bye to some o' the children and to old Margherita Corleone, the blind woman, and drove off in the carrier's van for Rome."

"And left no address?"

"Eh, what, address? *Perchè?* Ha! ha! She'll soon find a pleasant enough place in Rome, I'll warrant."

With that Torquil Bärnson's wish for antiquarian knowledge ceased. He was suddenly conscious of a great longing to see Rome once more. It was almost a week since he had been there!

Yes, there was the evening train. He had time to walk back to Marino, pack up his belongings, and catch *il ultimo convoglio*.

Action was welcome. Marino was reached as though he had skated thither on black ice. The bill was paid; *addios* were exchanged; finally, the train was caught.

That night, as he walked from his rooms in the Via delle Quattro Fontane, along the Via Sistina, to the antique fountain that throughout the year makes a joy of coolness and sound by the gates of the Pincio, he wondered what the morrow would bring forth. It was strange that in the falling music of the water which splashed and gurgled beneath the dense ilex-dome, even in the surging sigh that came up from the Piazza di Spagna and all *Roma oscura* beyond, he heard the same murmur as in the wind at Rocca di Papa, as in the wavelets lapping among the sedges of Lake Albano. *Bergliota*, came this murmur, *Bergliota — Bergliot — Fröken, Fröken Bergliot.*

In the morning he began his quest. No doubt this dawn-lover whom he had met in the woods of Tusculum would be up betimes; scarcely less doubt but that she would seek that high terrace whence sunrise may be seen as a pink rose unfolding over the white rose of Rome.

But as he walked to and fro in his solitary vigil, the idea suddenly occurred to him that Fröken Bergliot would far more likely hasten northward than linger in the city which sheltered also her Uncle Ernest.

Of course: what a fool he had been! Why, the north mail was due to leave in twenty minutes or so!

Three minutes later he was in a *vettura* and being driven at rattletrap speed towards the great gaunt station beyond the Baths of Diocletian.

It was five minutes to the time of starting when he alighted. A two-soldi platform ticket enabled him to pass the barrier. There, at the bookstall, he saw her: tall, beautiful, his goddess of the morning still.

"*Partenza!*" cried a guard, with premonitory urgency.

Torquil turned, aghast with a sudden reflection. He put his hand in his pocket. It was too true. There was a little silver in his right pocket; in the left, no purse. Both paper-money and his purse of gold were at his rooms. When he looked again, the girl had gone.

"Are you going by this train, signore?" asked a guard, imperatively.

"Yes; that is — no."

"Then I must ask you to leave the platform. His Royal Highness the Prince of Naples has just arrived, and is going to Florence by the express. The station is to be cleared. No, signore, you cannot go to the bookstall just now. Pray do not delay: go, I beg of you."

There was no help for it. But as Torquil

turned away he saw a small, old-fashioned brass-nail-studded box lying beside the luggage-wagon. His despairing eye caught at the name printed in large letters: BERGLIOT ROSS. In a second he stooped to note the address.

The label was in two parts. On the lower half, writ large, was "Hamburg." That, then, was her immediate destination. On the upper half he read, "Fröken Bergliot Ross, Bergen, Norvegia."

So absorbed was he that he did not at first notice the arrival of the royal party. When he did become aware of the fact, by the bustle around him, he saw what was more to the point, — his fresh opportunity.

The too attentive guard had disappeared. Swiftly walking forward, Torquil reached the bookstall. On the wooden shelf that projected from it, beside piles of the "Fanfulla," the "Popolo Romano," and other papers, was an earthenware jar containing a score of lovely tea-roses and ruby-red hearts-o'-love. To his right was a gentleman, who laid down a five-lire note, with the remark that he would have the roses "for the Prince." The newsvendor hesitated; the price was too low.

Torquil put down all the silver he had in his pocket, about twelve lire. "For the Princess," he said, and quietly walked off with the glory of roses.

Some died on the long northward journey; a few lingered and went seaward with the steamer that sailed from Hamburg; one, a deep, fragrant heart-o'-love, reached Bergen, and filled a little white room with its odour and beauty.

．　．　．　．　．　．　．　．　．

The hot autumn was followed by a lovely St. Martin's summer. Norway was bathed in a glow of gold and amber light by day, and veiled in starlit violet by night.

To be in Norway, to breathe this Norland air so loved and longed for, to rise in joy and fall asleep in peace amid all this home-sweet beauty, was to Fröken Bergliot a delight beyond words.

Only, by St. Martin's summer she was no longer Fröken Bergliot, but Frue Bergliot Bärnson.

www.ingramcontent.com/pod-product-compliance
Lightning Source LLC
Chambersburg PA
CBHW032112230426
43672CB00009B/1709